Serious Hours of a Young Lady

Charles Sainte-Foi

Contents

PREFACE. 7

CHAPTER I. IMPORTANCE OF THE TIME OF YOUTH; ....
DIFFICULTIES AND DANGERS THAT WOMEN MEET WITH IN LIFE, ...
AND THE NECESSITY OF PROVIDING FOR THEM. 9

CHAPTER II. ILLUSIONS OF YOUTH, VALUE OF TIME AT ....
THIS PERIOD OF LIFE. 14

CHAPTER III. THE HEART OF WOMAN; THE NECESSITY OF ....
REGULATING IT DURING YOUTH. 19

CHAPTER IV. THE DIGNITY OF WOMAN. 24

CHAPTER V. EVE AND MARY. 29

CHAPTER VI. EVE AND MARY CONTINUED. 34

CHAPTER VII. THE WORLD. 40

CHAPTER VIII. THE SAME SUBJECT CONTINUED. 45

CHAPTER IX. THE WILL. 49

CHAPTER X. THE IMAGINATION. 55

CHAPTER XI. PIETY. 60

CHAPTER XII. VOCATION. 66

CHAPTER XIII. A SERIOUS MIND. 72

CHAPTER XIV. CHOICE OP COMPANIONS. 78

CHAPTER XV. TOILET. 82

CHAPTER XVI. DESIRE TO PLEASE. 86

CHAPTER XVII. CURIOSITY. 92

CHAPTER XVIII. MEDITATION AND REFLECTION. 96

CHAPTER XIX. OBEDIENCE TO PARENTS. 101

CHAPTER XX. MELANCHOLY. 107

CHAPTER XXI. ON READING. 112

CHAPTER XXII. SAME SUBJECT CONTINUED. 117

SERIOUS HOURS OF A YOUNG LADY

BY

Charles Sainte-Foi

PREFACE.

A celebrated author has justly remarked that Christian women can, like the guardian angels, invisibly govern the world; and the author of the " *Serious Hours of a Young Lady*" has very appropriately made this truth the basis of his book, since the object that he had in view in writing it was to point out the important role that woman plays in society, and to give the young girl such instructions as will enable her, in due time, to discharge, in a worthy manner, the duties of her calling. In doing this he has given evidence of very elevated views and of a profound knowledge of the human heart. The book is a tissue of practical counsels, couched in the clearest and most delicate terms.

Hence, judging from its intrinsic worth, and the universal welcome with which it has been hailed in the original, we feel that it is no exaggeration to assert that it has rendered and will still render inestimable good to society.

After having lucidly exposed the importance of woman's mission in this world, and pointed out the evils that prevent its realization, the author ingeniously brings before the mind's eye the different phases of her life, the varied process of development that she undergoes in all her faculties, the dangerous influences to which she is constantly exposed, the means that should be employed to ensure her protection.

We behold her on the threshold of childhood a tiny, timid and retiring creature, naturally disposed to attach her affections to all that is pure and elevated, to everything that conduces to the practice of virtue and the love of God. While yet a child she is the little confidante and angel of consolation of her brothers and sisters in their pains and difficulties. At a more advanced age we see her consoling her aged parents in their sorrows and afflictions; and when she merges into womanhood she becomes either the spouse of Jesus Christ or of man, only to continue the same work of beneficence in some charitable asylum, or in the midst of domestic cares. But ere she attains this last stage of life how numerous and great are the difficulties that she must encounter, the dangers to which she will be exposed, and the snares to entrap her!

Hence, to ensure her safety and prepare her to act the important role that she holds in society, her education must be the work of piety, modesty and retirement. All that interferes with their action in her soul must be peremptorily removed. Worldly pleasures with their numerous cortège should never have access to the sanctuary of her heart, for their poisoned influence blasts the fairest flower in her crown of simplicity. But, alas! we confess, with deep regret, that there are many thoughtless tutors who seemingly ignore the grave responsibility of their charge, and unwarrantably parade the little one before the world's gaze, which creates in the heart evil impressions, frivolous tastes and inordinate desires. And, even when they would all prove faithful to their trust, it is a noted fact that society, friends and companions wield a powerful influence over the mind and heart of a young girl, which, when allowed to continue, most invariably proves pernicious to her spiritual and temporal welfare.

Hence, she stands in need of a true friend, a faithful adviser, on whom she can depend for safe instruction, and to whom she can have recourse as often as need be. The "*Serious Hours*" is unquestionably all this; it speaks openly, firmly, but mildly. It inspires the young girl with that genuine, lofty esteem that she should have for herself and for the dignity of her sex. It clearly defines her line of conduct in all the most critical incidents and circumstances of life, so that she cannot be deceived unless that she wilfully shuts her eyes to the light of truth. It is all that the author proposed to make it, a first class book of instruction for young ladies, showing a careful study of all their wants and a happy choice of the remedies to meet them. And, believing that such a valuable book ought to be made accessible to all nations, we have ventured to present it to the public in an English dress. How far we have succeeded in rendering both its form and spirit we leave the public to decide. And, while we are fully aware that, in transferring the genius of one language to another, some of the original delicate shades of beauty must be inevitably sacrificed--the present translation not excepted--still we are happy to say that the work was one of love and deep interest to us, on account of its importance and good to society.

CHAPTER I.
IMPORTANCE OF THE TIME OF YOUTH; DIFFICULTIES AND DANGERS THAT WOMEN MEET WITH IN LIFE, AND THE NECESSITY OF PROVIDING FOR THEM.

The most important period of life is that in which we are the better able, in making good use of the present, to repair the past and prepare for the future; that period holds the intermediate place between the age of infancy and the age of maturity, embracing the advantages of both, presenting at the same time the flowers of the one with the fruits of the other. In order to prepare for the future we need a certain assistance from the past, for this preparation demands a certain maturity of judgment and a force of will that experience alone can give.

The child, devoid as it is of personal experience, can, by turning that of others to good account, make up for the deficiencies of its youth, and prepare for the future without having to learn in the severe school of self-experience. But, through an unfortunate occurrence of circumstances, and very often without any fault of theirs, the greater part of children attain the age of manhood and womanhood without having reaped the precious advantages offered them by the first stage of life, when the soul is most susceptible of receiving the impress of grace and virtue. A vitiated or inadequate primitive education, bad example, pernicious instruction? perchance, or at least personal levity of character, combined with that of childhood, deprive this age of many advantages, and call for a total reparation of the past, at a period of life that should be the living figure of hope.

Happy, indeed, are those who have only the levity and negligences of childhood to repair, and who have never felt the crushing weight of a humiliating and grievous fault! Alas! that purity, that innocence so common formerly among children, is every day disappearing from their midst, many among them have become the victims of sin ere the passions of the heart manifested their presence; and their hearts have quivered from the sting of remorse ere they felt the perfidious lurings of pleasure. Many have received from sin that doleful experience, that premature craftiness, which, far from enlightening the mind, obscures and blinds it,--which, far from fortifying the will, enfeebles and enervates it.

Such is the light by which we can truly see the importance that should be attached to the time of youth. At this period of life sin has not yet taken deep root in the heart,--it has not at least assumed the frightful magnitude of one of those inveterate habits, justly called habits of second nature, which invade and pollute the sacred sanctuary of both body and soul, forming in the earliest instincts, inclinations and desires so violent, so obstinate, that superhuman efforts with a life-long struggle are the consequences entailed upon the unfortunate victims, who desire to hold them in subjection.

However, it is invariably true that, if the passions peculiar to youth virulently assail virtue and expose the heart to the seductions of pleasure, they also give a great facility of doing good, by inflaming youthful zeal which age never fails to cool. The ardor aroused by them for the commission of evil can be easily employed for the practice of virtue; they are young and fiery steeds which God has placed at your disposal, ready to obey your orders. Attach them to the chariot of your will, they will not fail to draw you in the direction that you may open to their impetuosity. It matters not to them whether they run upon the way of vice or virtue,--all that they require is to go, to run and not to be constrained to inaction, which kills them. They must be managed by a resolute will which holds the reins with a firm grip, and by a calm intelligence, skilled to direct them.

Trees, while young, can be easily plied into any direction that man may wish to give them. The same may be said of hearts in which the frost of age has not cooled the ardor and impetuosity of desire. Their energy and vivacity, whether for good or evil, never forsake them. They are like those spirited racers which are no sooner down than up again, for, swift as a flash, they will turn you to God by repentance and love, the moment you have the misfortune of losing Him by sin. Be then full of confidence and hope, young soul, to whom God has opened with a liberal hand the spring-time of life; be grateful to Him for so signal a favor, and, like a wise econo- mist, profit by the resources that He places at your disposal. But, should the past recall some doleful memories, be not dismayed; be hopeful and, re- animating your courage, prepare for the future by sowing at present the germs of those beautiful virtues which grace irrigates, and whose fruits will rejoice your old age and atone for the sterility of your earlier years.

Your future happiness is insured if you fully comprehend the importance of the epoch which you now begin, and the greatness of its results for the rest of your life. Let past delinquencies become an incentive, stimulating your will to energetic action. Let the need of repairing the past, and the importance of preparing for the future inspire you with generous resolutions and an ardent desire of acquiring all the virtues necessary to a person of your sex and position, in order that you may discharge in a worthy manner all the duties which may be required of you. Regard the future with a calm and firm eye, without exaggerating the difficulties, but also without dissembling the dangers. The first condition required to avoid a danger is to know it, for the ignorance that conceals from us the snares which we should avoid is--after the evil inclination that leads us into them--man's greatest misfortune, and the most disastrous of the effects of original sin.

Women, even in the most humble walks of life, can scarcely hope now-a-days to enjoy that sweet, calm and peaceful life which was formerly insured by the pur- est morals and the most pious customs.

If the world, spite of that inordinate desire for reform and innovation which consumes it, has not yet seriously endeavored to withdraw woman from the circle to which Providence would have her devote the activity of her mind and life; if it has consented till now to have her shun the theatre and the whirlpool of politi- cal commotions, it will be extremely difficult for her to escape its counter-shock, and preserve her self-composure and serenity of soul in the midst of those turbu- lent events which absorb her husband's life, that of her children, of her father and brothers. If it was easy for her to preserve her heart at a tender age from the seduc- tions of the world and the dangerous snares of vanity or pleasure, through the sweet influence of those more modest, and at the same time more rigid customs which identified her thoughts and affections with the family circle; such is not the case at present, for an unfortunate necessity, invested with the vain title of propriety, compels her to seek in a more fashionable, a more numerous, and consequently an unsuitable society, distractions or pastimes for which she is not made, and which recreate neither body, nor mind, nor heart.

The feverish agitation and insatiable thirst for enjoyment which seem to prevail among all ages and classes of the present day is enigmatical. Life now-a-days must be passed in a state of constant excitement. The peaceful calm productive of a modest and pure life appear to the imagination like a monotonous and disdainful sleep. The young girl herself has scarcely left the paternal home in which she passed her youthful days when she dreams of the pleasing emotions and incomparable joys promised her by a flashy and fashionable life. The examples which come under her notice wherever she goes or wherever she turns her eyes,--the language which she hears, and the very air which she breathes,--all give her, as it were, a foretaste of the false pleasures which now fascinate her imagination.

This is, most assuredly, one of the worst signs of our time. Up to the present day women, for the most part, faithful to their vocation and to the duties of their station in life, have carefully preserved in the family circle that sacred fire of Christian virtue which forms magnanimous souls, and that piety which produces saints. Their hearts, like the Ark of the Covenant, have preserved intact those tables of the divine law which admonish men of their duties, and inspire them with a firm hope. They have not fixed their hearts on the vain and frivolous joys of earth; no, heaven was their aim. Preserved from the contagion of worldly interests and desires, their thoughts feasted on elevated and heavenly objects. What will become of society if, deprived of the resources it found in their virtues, it meets with no other barrier on the steep declivity down which it is being impelled by cupidity and the love of pleasure? What will be the fate of future generations if they are not sanctified in the sanctuary of the family by the benevolent influence of woman, and fortified against the seductions of vice by that odor of grace and sanctity which the heart of a Christian mother exhales?

Be not discouraged at the sight of difficulties that hover over the horizon of the future; on the contrary, they should inspire you with greater courage and energy. The less help you will obtain from trusted sources of reliance, the more earnestly should you seek in God and yourself what you look for in vain elsewhere. You may expect to see diminish, from day to day, the number of those saintly souls from whom you could obtain advice, support or light.

For you, perhaps, like many others, life will be a desert which you must traverse almost alone, without meeting a single soul to reach you a helping hand in your necessities and trials. Being about to set out on this pilgrimage of life, which will perhaps be long, fatiguing and painful, be supplied with an ample provision of strength, patience, virtue and energy. And, if happily deceived in your fears, you find the road which leads to eternity smooth under your feet, you will at least have the merit of having been wise in your conduct, for not less moral strength is required to bear the happiness of prosperity than the misfortune of adversity. Happiness here below is something so extremely perilous to man's eternal welfare that few can taste it without injury to their souls. Hence, in order to guard against its fatal influence, not less preparation, nor less time, nor less efforts, are required than to suffer the privations imposed by adversity, for experience proves that the former is more destructive than the latter to the work of eternal salvation.

CHAPTER II.
ILLUSIONS OF YOUTH, VALUE OF TIME AT THIS PERIOD OF LIFE.

The age of youth is the age of illusions, ardent desires, and fanciful hopes. Youth is like a fairy whose magical wand evokes the most graceful images and the most alluring phantoms. This ignorance of the doleful realities concealed in the future is a gift of divine goodness which, in order that life might not be too bitter, casts a beneficent veil over the sorrows that await us; God screens the future from us to let us enjoy the present. Far be it from me to remove this veil which renders you such kind service. But, apart from this screen which the good God has placed between you and the miseries of this life, there is another of a darker and heavier shade, fabricated by the imagination, and which it draws with a perfidious complacency over the object which it behooves us the most to know and avoid--a seductive and deceitful veil which, while presenting things to us in a false light, exposes us to most deplorable illusions and inevitable dangers.

God permits that we should ignore many things, but He does not wish that we should be deceived in anything. He is truth itself; error can never claim His acquiescence.

If prudence and respect for God's work make it a duty for me to leave intact the veil that He has drawn between you and the future, I would consider it highly criminal in me if I did not endeavor to remove that by which your imagination seeks to conceal its illusions and its errors. It is not my wish or design to trouble the present by exaggerated anxiety; but, on the other hand, I do not wish to leave you under a false impression, fed by delusive hopes relative to the future. My desire is that, while enjoying with gratitude and simplicity the happiness or peace which God has bestowed upon you in the springtime of life, you may profit by the calm and tranquillity it affords you to prepare for the future, and to anticipate a means of soothing its sorrows and bitterness.

While the soil of your heart is yet untilled and moist, and while your hands are yet filled with those heavenly seeds which God has given you in abundance, I desire that you may sow them in the light and strength of divine grace, to develop in them the heavenly germs which they contain, that you may be enabled to reap at a later time an abundant harvest of virtues, holy joy and merit before God and men. I desire that you may learn to turn to good account all the natural resources that you possess, and acquire that knowledge of yourself which enlightens the mind without troubling the heart; I do not wish to discourage nor flatter you, I only wish to instruct and fortify you.

Do not think that the river of life will always flow for you as it does at present, broad, deep, calm and limpid, between two flowery banks. Age will diminish those waters and deprive their banks of their charm and freshness. The flame of passion, like a burning wind, will rise, and more than once perhaps will bring to the surface the mud that rankles in the bottom, and thus destroy its limpidity.

A day will come, and before long, when, stripped of all those exterior advantages which please the senses, you will possess only those qualities, less striking, but more solid, which satisfy the mind and heart and attract the complaisant regard of God and the angels. Youth will quickly pass, more quickly than you think, and the subsequent period of life will last much longer, hence, in all justice to yourself, let its preparation absorb your attention.

If you had a long sojourn to make in a place close by, would it be reasonable on your part to pay less attention to the place of your destination than to the few fleeting moments it would require to go thither. Youth is not a stopping-place, it is a passage, a time of preparation; it is to the whole life what the florid period is to the gardener, or seed-time to the farmer.

Oh! if you did but fully comprehend the value of each hour during this most important period of life, the value of each thought of your mind, of each sentiment of your heart, with what extreme care you would watch over all the movements of your soul, nay, even the external movements of your body.

That fugitive thought which enters your mind, fanned by curiosity's wing, may seem quite trivial; to dwell on and delight in it may be to you something indifferent. That sentiment which, scarcely formed, commences to germinate in your heart, and to produce therein emotions so imperceptible that you are but imperfectly conscious of its presence, seems insignificant at first sight; that unguarded glance seemed to you a matter of no import, and which, at an earlier or later period of your life, would have but little consequence. At an earlier age the impression, it is true, would be lively but inconsistent, and the levity of childhood would soon have replaced it by another; later it would be found so superficial and trivial that it would be soon forgotten among the multiplicity of thoughts which absorb the mind at the age of maturity; but, during the youthful years, everything that comes under the notice of the senses sinks deeply into the soul, penetrating its very substance, the faculties still retain all the vivacity of youth, while already they participate in that firmness which is characteristic of the age of maturity.

That thought is, perhaps, the first link in a chain of thoughts and images which will be the torment of your conscience and the bane of your life. That sentiment to which you imprudently pandered is perhaps the source of countless fears, regrets, remorse and sorrows. That imprudent glance is perhaps the first spark of a conflagration which nothing can extinguish, and which will destroy your brightest hopes.

If, as yet, you are ignorant of all the evil of which an imprudent glance may be productive, recall to mind the example furnished us by the Sacred Scriptures in the person of David, who, for his imprudent glance at the wife of Urias, committed two crimes, the names of which you should ignore, and suffered a life of sorrow, repentance, bitterness and anguish: a life which even yet serves to express the sorrow and repentance of imprudent souls who have yielded to the allurements of the senses. And, nevertheless, David had attained the age of discretion when the mind is firm and the will is strong; David was the cherished one of God; he was just and virtuous, one on whom God had special designs of mercy. What a terrible example! What a severe, but at the same time instructive, lesson!

Young Christian soul, may it never be your sad experience to learn the effect of an imprudent glance which would exact from you the bitter wages of countless tears and regrets. Is there anything in the material world so beautiful, so beneficent as the light and heat that we receive from the sun; is there among material things a livelier image of the goodness of God towards us? And, nevertheless, let the sun shine upon the young and tender flower or vine immediately after a shower of rain, and it will cause them to droop and wither. The reason is quite obvious, for at no time is a being so frail and delicate as at the moment of its formation. There is a critical period for all beings, during which the greatest possible care is necessary. In this relation, what is said of the body may be said of the soul; character is formed and developed according to the same laws which regulate the development of the physical constitution.

Are you not aware of the extraordinary care that must be taken of those organs that are the chief motors of the body, while they are under process of development? Are you not aware that the fresh air which you inhale and which purifies and invigorates the blood contains for you the germ of death, which justifies in your good parents the anxious care they take of your health, but which you perhaps regard as entirely unnecessary?

Now, what the lungs are to the human body, that the heart is to the soul. It is by the heart that we breathe the spiritual and divine atmosphere that sustains our moral life. This atmosphere is composed of three elements,--truth, goodness and beauty, which envelop and penetrate the soul's substance; as it is the respiratory organ of the mind it follows that for the heart, as well as for the lungs, there is an epoch of development which is dangerous, and which, consequently, demands the greatest possible care; it is the epoch of your age at present. An emotion too vivid, an indiscreet thought, an imprudent glance, is quite sufficient to imperil the interesting and delicate process by which your moral constitution is formed, to accelerate the development of the heart, and thus give to this most important organ a pernicious precocity or a false direction.

Your mother, anxious and always trembling for your welfare, guards it with tender solicitude from all the dangers to which it might be exposed. But her vigilance cannot equal that of your guardian angel, nor the care with which he removes you from contact with all that might in any way tarnish the purity of your soul, or trouble its peace and harmony. It is to you that the Holy Ghost addresses these words of the Proverbs: With all watchfulness keep thy heart, because life issueth out from it.[1]

The heart is, therefore, the seat of the moral life, and as the source is known by the waters that flow from it, so will the moral life partake of the character and bear the impress of the heart whence it proceeds. This is true of youth in general, but more particularly so of young ladies.

---

1   Proverbs iv 23.

CHAPTER III.
THE HEART OF WOMAN; THE NECESSITY OF REGULATING IT DURING YOUTH.

The most humble, most chaste, most holy of women, Blessed Mary ever Virgin, she who is the ornament and glory of her sex who, in consequence of her privilege of being the mother of God, merited to be elevated so high above all creatures, revealed to us the existence of a faculty in the soul, unknown to the philosophers, undiscovered by the saints, unspoken of by the prophets. This faculty is more conspicuous in woman than in man, for it exercises in her a decisive influence which extends over the entire period of her life. Hence, God, "who ordereth all things, sweetly," (Wisdom, viii. 1), desired that its existence should be made known to us by a woman, and that, too, while she was visiting another woman.

In answer to the salutation of her cousin St. Elizabeth, Mary, filled with the Holy Ghost, breaks forth into that sublime Canticle, called the "Magnificat:" "He hath scattered the proud," she sings, "*mente cordis sui;*" literally, "in the *mind* of their heart." This is the faculty of which I speak; that *mind*, that *intellect of the heart*, if I may so term it, which is the hidden recess, the secret chamber of the soul, either blessed by the peaceful presence of humility, or cursed by the baneful restlessness of worldly ambition or pride.

It is not going too far to say that a woman's mind is in her heart; it is the source both of the thoughts which ennoble and elevate, and of those which are selfish and worldly; it is the key to all the powers of her soul, so that he who becomes the possessor of her heart is master of her whole being, and can exercise over her a power of fascination which has no parallel in nature.

God who disposes every being for the end which He proposed to Himself in creating it has established in woman's heart an abyss which no human affection can fill nor exhaust when once it has been filled, because He desired to submerge her whole being in love, and thus to render easy and necessary to her the noblest sentiments and the most heroic sacrifices. Such is the agent that He wished to employ for the culture of charity in society and in the family circle, as well as of the virtues of tenderness, compassion and devotedness. He desired that in the family the child should be borne, so to speak, on woman's heart and man's intelligence, as on the two arms of one and the same being; He desired that in society the mind of the one should furnish the light to guide in the way, and the love of the other should produce that vivifying principle which animates and quickens man's being: And, thus, that the moral life of humanity should be the result of these two factors. God endowed the heart of woman with treasures of tenderness and devotedness, desiring to be Himself the supreme object of its devotion. To Himself alone has He reserved the power of calming its fearful agitation and soothing its poignant grief, hence we see it turning to Him in its joys and sorrows, like the magnet to the pole that attracts it. He has made the heart of woman broad and deep, so that its devotedness may suffice for all the exigencies it is called upon to meet, whether in society or in the family, yet finding no created object able to exhaust it.

When, forgetting the sublime end for which she has been created, woman lives for the world and not for heaven, lavishing her love on creatures instead of giving it to God, her Creator, her soul becomes the prey of inexpressible anguish and despondency, which admonish her of her mistake and induce her to correct it.

You can easily judge from this of what great importance it is to you to keep a vigilant watch over your heart and its movements, since the heart is, so to speak, the citadel of your whole being, and hence when it is captured all the powers and faculties of your soul are forced to surrender. The heart is the agent that furnishes woman with the greater part of her ideas, and the object of its predilection inevitably becomes the only object of all her thoughts. This is the artist that furnishes the imagination with those images which remain substantially the same under forms constantly varying, but absorbing the soul to such a degree that a person is often tempted to look upon their action as the result of obsession.

It is the heart that governs and shapes the will, giving it that flexibility and at the same time that constancy so prevalent among the greater part of women, leading them, with unflinching stubbornness of determination to the accomplishment of the end proposed. All difficulties vanish that stand between them and the object of their heart. This disposition renders them potent for good or evil, hence the necessity of regulating the heart and of never losing control over its movements. When their soul is swayed by a pure and generous sentiment, and when the natural weakness of their sex gives place to an energy which few men are capable of displaying, their ardor in doing good is truly admirable. God alone knows all the treasures of virtue stored up within them daily, by charity, maternal love, filial piety, devotedness and compassion, but He alone also knows the malicious excess to which a sentiment, bad in its nature or in its source, may lead them.

Oh, if while standing between these two abysses of good and evil, you could sound their depth, and behold the ineffable joy and glory that women have secured by the practice of virtue, the sorrow, disgust, humiliation and shame that evil doings have brought upon them (faults which at first sight did not seem capable of entailing such fatal consequences) horror and admiration should dispute the possession of your soul; you would indeed tremble on beholding the consequences of neglecting your vocation, while you would be astonished at the sublime elevation that fidelity to grace would secure to you in heaven.

God desires to accomplish great things through your instrumentality, and in order to secure your services with greater certainty he has placed around you barriers which you cannot pass without an effort that does violence to nature, still necessity makes it a duty to break them down, and necessity has no law. When the first step is taken nothing can impede the will in the execution of your designs, be they good or bad. Hence the great importance of making your first step in the right direction, as it will be the prelude to countless others.

If you wish to possess your own heart and insure to yourself a life exempt from trouble and remorse, attach it firmly to God; accustom it to always prefer duty to pleasure and to propose to itself in all its movements an end worthy of your sublime destiny. Remember that God alone can satisfy it--no creature being able to give it that peace which it so ardently craves. O, my child, if you knew the gnawing desires, the vain hopes, the false joys, the troubles, the regrets and bitterness that fill the heart in which God does not dwell! If your eyes were not screened by the veil of candor and simplicity preventing you from foreseeing the torments to which that woman's life is exposed, who has not learned in early youth to regulate the desires and affections of her heart, you would better understand my words, and the necessity of laboring energetically and efficiently to direct your own, and to check all its irregular movements. Learn now, and profit by the experience of others. Hearken to the voice of God addressing you in these words: "The flowers have appeared in our land, the time of pruning is come; the voice of the turtle is heard in our land; the vines in flower yield their sweet smell. Arise, my love, and come. Catch us the little foxes that destroy the vines, for our vineyard hath flourished." (Cant. ch. ii. 12, 13, 15). The foxes of which the sacred writer speaks here are those defects which, although they appear small, still assail the soul with great virulence, and will leave no virtue intact unless you hasten to destroy them.

The time for pruning is the time of youth, age truly precious wherein you can still lop off useless branches which absorb a portion of the sap, depriving the others of that strength which they need in order to produce an abundance of savory fruit. You should attack not only those gross and manifest defects which disfigure the soul, but also those imperfections which are slight in appearance, but which, if left alone, will in time become pernicious inclinations. You should even watch over certain natural dispositions, which, though good in themselves, and even often esteemed above their true merit by the world, might easily, on that account, divert the thoughts of the mind and the efforts of the will from more important objects; dispositions very often dangerous for those who possess them, because it is easy to abuse them, and because they flatter and nourish self-love, or the other passions that flesh is heir to. You should imitate those intelligent gardeners who pay a daily visit to their garden, pruning knife in hand, and cut off branches that might exhaust or overcharge the tree--not sparing them for the beauty of their foliage or the brightness of their flowers.

If you wish to cultivate your heart and make it produce all the fruit and virtue that it is capable of producing, suffer nothing useless or superfluous to grow therein, choosing what is best, measuring your esteem of certain things, and your application of certain duties by the degree of importance that each merits, giving the preference, in your mind and heart, to the virtues which bring the soul nearest to God. Love those hidden virtues, so modest and humble, which are the ornament of your sex--those virtues of which God alone is witness, which the world ignores,--which it often, in fact, despises, because they secure no advantage in men's esteem, receiving their reward only in the future world. But this is just the reason why God loves them so dearly, and why you should prefer them. For if, in general, it is dangerous to please the world and useful to shun it, this truth is especially applicable to woman, who, being confined to a narrower sphere, and devoted to more intimate affections than man, is obliged to seek, at a tender age, isolation, tranquillity, repose, and that retirement which are truly a shield to her virtues. In this way you will do more for the real development and culture of your heart than by the acquisition of more agreeable and more brilliant qualities.

Moreover, the same thing will happen for you that always happens when efforts are made to acquire what is best; when that which is essential is secured, the accessories will infallibly follow, just as the effect follows the cause that produces it. By acquiring the virtues that are pleasing to God you will receive, in addition, those which men esteem; in becoming more and more agreeable to God you will become more and more pleasing to men, whose good sense and sound judgment almost invariably triumph over prejudice which an austere but modest virtue always removes. This is also what the Saviour of the world insinuates by these words of the Gospel in which He recommends us to seek first the kingdom of God and His justice, promising that all other things shall be added thereto. But this addition should not be directly sought, nor should it be ardently desired; await the will of God who has promised it to us, provided that we first seek the things to which that is accessory. Very often, on the contrary, when, through want of due reflection, preference is given to secondary and inferior things, by neglecting solid and hidden virtues for brilliant qualities, neither are obtained. God permits this in order to punish this subversion of the moral order and of the laws that govern it.

CHAPTER IV.
THE DIGNITY OF WOMAN.

POPE ST. LEO, in one of his homilies on the nativity of our Saviour, says, in addressing man: "O man, recognize thy dignity!" We might, with all due propriety, address these same words to woman, for her happiness and virtues depend in great measure on the elevated idea that she has of herself, and on the care with which she maintains this idea, both in her own mind and in that of others. Woe to the woman who, through false modesty, or something still worse, has lost self-respect, for she has deprived herself of her most powerful safeguard against instability of character and seductions of the world.

Woman has received from God the sublime mission of fostering in society the spirit of sacrifice and devotedness. Faithful, nay, sometimes perhaps over-zealous, in the discharge of these duties, she feels an imperative need of sacrificing herself to another who should constitute the complement of her life. As long as she has not made this surrender of herself to another she is a burden to herself, for she seems to find her liberty and happiness in this voluntary servitude of the heart, in this constant abnegation, in this perpetual sacrifice of her whole being.

This disposition of woman's heart, which has been given her for the good of society and for her own happiness, can be easily used to the detriment of both; such is necessarily the case the moment she sinks in her own estimation, so as to account herself a being of little value. It is a matter of vital importance to her to have a just idea of the value of the present she is making when she engages her heart and her fidelity. In fact, when a thing is lightly appreciated, we make little account of giving it away and less of choosing those to whom we give it. Now, if we consider the deplorable facility with which a vast number of women obey the caprice of their heart or of their imagination, we will be led to conclude that their valuation of them--selves is very low indeed. They seem to lose sight of the fact that in giving their heart they give the key to all the treasures that enrich their soul; they give their will, all their thoughts, their whole life. They sometimes give more than all this, they give their eternal salvation, their conscience, and God Himself, putting in His place, by a sort of idolatry, the object that claims their heart.

To prevent this deplorable prodigality of themselves, women should spare no pains to comprehend thoroughly their dignity, of which they can never have too high an appreciation or too great an esteem. It would be most prejudicial to them to lower in their own mind their just value by a false humility.

The most humble of all women is, at the same time, she who had the best knowledge of her dignity. And her humility, which was never equaled by that of any other woman, did not hinder her from seeing the great things that God had operated in her, as she herself proclaims in that sublime canticle which is the "Magna Charta" of the rights, the prerogatives and the greatness of woman.

The two most beautiful and most elevated things in all creation are the intelligence of man and, the heart of woman. They are the special objects of God's complacency. He seems to be absorbed in the work of their education; to this end he seems to have converged all the miracles wrought by His divine Son, all the mysteries of Jesus Christ.

To impart to man a knowledge of truth and a love of virtue was the end that God proposed to Himself in the creation of the world. But the order which he had established was iniquitously subverted, and this subversion has shaken society to its very foundation, leading man's intelligence to conceive a hatred for truth and to become the slave of error; turning away the heart of woman from what is truly good and great to pander to false and transitory goods, which sully without contenting it.

The heart of woman may be said to be the source from which flows all the good or evil that consoles or afflicts mankind. As the city and state receive their form and character from the family, so the family is modelled after the type of the mother's heart, since upon her devolves the culture of the infant mind, that all-important education upon which depends man's weal or woe, both for time and eternity. Hence it is that, while writing this little work, and considering that many to whom it is addressed will read its pages, namely those who are destined to be one day heads of families, charged with the education of several children, who in turn will found numerous families to act a more or less important part in the great movement by which the plan of divine Providence is executed throughout ages, I feel a kind of profound respect, bordering on reverential awe, that engages me to pray God to inspire me with thoughts equal to the sublimity of my subject.

Whoever you may be that read and meditate this little book, I honor and venerate the dignity of your vocation; I regard you as an august and sacred being. I admire the great designs that God has over you; I pray Him to have you participate in the sovereign esteem and respect with which your condition inspires me. You are as yet free from all engagements, in the bloom of youth, adorned with the treasures of innocence and candor, standing like a queen upon the threshold of the future which opens before you like a spacious temple. The past is immaculate and free from the sting of remorse; with a vigorous mind and will you behold the future's perspective without anxiety or dismay,--rich in pious souvenirs, saintly hopes, heavenly thoughts and merits acquired by prayer and the practice of virtue, ignorant of vice and its bitter consequences, save by the pictures that have been painted in order to inspire you with horror for it; your liberty is such that every Christian soul envies your happy state. You possess a power--I would almost say, a majesty--that no one can help admiring and revering. As there is no one freer than he who has never been the slave of sin, so there is no man stronger than he who has never succumbed to the allurements of pleasure. The woof of your life is there spread out before you intact and flexible, you can dispose and weave it as you please; you will now find none of those knotty or broken threads which, in after life, must sometimes be met with.

You are now at the period of life at which all the roads of life meet. You can choose the one that pleases you most, and enter on the good way with all that generous ardor so natural to youth. But, whatever you do, whatever the choice you may make, you will occasion the future weal or woe of many, perhaps for many generations. Whether spouse of Jesus Christ or of man, whether mother of a family or of the poor, whether a cloistered nun or a celibate in the world, you will neither save nor lose your soul alone; the effects of your virtues or vices shall be reproduced, long after your departure from the scene of life, in the lives of beings yet unborn, in favor of whom divine Providence implores your compassion. What a solemn moment! What sublime power! Have you given it serious thought?

Transport yourself, in thought, to the house of Nazareth, recall to mind the day on which Gabriel proposed to your Queen to become the mother of God, asking her consent to the Incarnation, by which was to be accomplished the salvation of the world. The angel's words astonished Mary's humility so far as to make her recoil before such a prodigious elevation, and, to obtain her consent, it was necessary to assure her that the Holy Ghost Himself would accomplish in her this prodigy. Indeed, it was a most memorable moment in the world's history,--a moment wherein the salvation of the entire human race hung upon the word of a virgin's lips.

Now, in your present condition, at this period of your life, you bear a certain resemblance to the Blessed Virgin at Nazareth, on the day of the Annunciation. A glorious destiny is also announced to you; to you also is promised a saintly posterity, if you give your consent and concurrence to the Holy Ghost, with docility to the operation of His grace. Be not astonished at so great an honor. The choice that you are going to make, the course that you are going to adopt, will determine and fix the fate of a family, of a generation,--of many generations perhaps, for God alone can tell how far the influence of your virtues or the result of your faults may extend.

If you have no regard for your own salvation or glory, oh, at least have pity for those whom the hand of God will place under your care, to be modeled by your instructions and example. Have compassion on them and on those who, succeeding them, must inherit your virtues or vices. Oh! how pleasing to God and respected of men is the young lady who, piously impressed with the greatness of her vocation, prepares for the future in a Christian manner, and resolves courageously to embrace and faithfully to discharge all its duties.

Like Mary, the model and glory of your sex, you also, but in a spiritual manner, are carrying Jesus Christ within you; and He, by the operation of the Holy Ghost, is leaving the impress of His virtues in your soul, that one day you may give Him birth spiritually, producing Him externally by a pure and Christian life. Like her you should be ready to accomplish the will of God in your own regard, saying, as she did, with sentiments of obedience and profound humility: "***Behold the handmaid of the Lord, be it done unto me according to Thy word;***" abandoning your soul with perfect docility to the operation of the Holy Ghost, following Him wherever He desires to lead you. Let your soul glorify God, and rejoice in Him on account of the great things He has done in you, remembering that His mercy extends from generation to generation, in favor of those who fear him, and that holy families, fearing God, are formed by the lessons and examples of virtuous, God-fearing women. He reduces to naught those who confide in their own power and strength, while He sustains and exalts the humble. He freely shares His treasures with those who desire them, and reduces to indigence those who glory in their own abundance.

Let this beautiful canticle dwell in your heart and be the prayer of your lips; in this canticle, composed by the Mother of God, the honor and glory of your sex, or rather by the Holy Ghost Himself, who inspired her, He has inscribed all the rights and glories of women, by celebrating in it the power of her feebleness, the greatness of her humility and of all those modest virtues which so well become your condition.

A Christian woman who would never lose sight of what she is, of her worth, of her moral capabilities and of her sacred duties, will find in the frequent meditation of this sublime canticle considerations suggestive of thoughts and sentiments corresponding to God's designs over her. She should nourish her soul with the vivifying substance of the words it contains, and look therein for light to dispel her doubts, and for consolation in her troubles. In them she will also find a cheering hope in her languor, a powerful prayer in temptation, an acceptable act of thanksgiving, and a hymn of joy and triumph in her victories.

CHAPTER V.
EVE AND MARY.

PILATE, on presenting to the Jews, Jesus crowned with thorns, and clothed in a purple garment, said: "*Behold the Man!*" Jesus frequently calls Himself the Son of man in the Gospel, that is, the Man *par excellence*, the Man who is the model and type of all others. To women, we can also say of Mary: "*Behold the woman!*" the honor, glory, joy, crown, type and model of your sex. Such is the manner in which Jesus presented her from the cross on Calvary, when He said to her, a few moments before expiring: "*Woman, behold thy Son!*"

It is, indeed, remarkable that the Saviour of the world, when addressing Mary in public, did not call her mother, but woman, as if, by that, He would declare to us that she is the model of all other women. It is as if He said to us: Behold THE woman; and, although she was His mother--principal title of her glory--nevertheless she is woman before all. She merited to become the most glorious of all mothers only because she had been the purest and holiest of all women. You should therefore have your eyes constantly fixed upon Mary, as a servant who watches her mistress in order to observe and obey her commands. If you can see yourself in Mary, you will entertain an exalted idea of the dignity of your sex; for it is in her and by her that you are great; it is to her you owe the honor and respect that the world pays the woman who knows how to respect and appreciate herself according to her just value. If you would understand all that you owe to Mary in this regard you need but consider what was the social condition of woman in society before the birth of Christ, and what her condition is to-day among people on whom the light of the Gospel has not yet shone. You are now too young to appeal to your own experience, but, according as you advance in life, observing closely what passes around you, you will learn--and God grant that it may not be at your own expense--what an immense difference there is with regard to the esteem in which woman is held between those who adore God as the Son of Mary, and those who regard her as common with other women.

Among men of social standing, whose habits, condition and character are so different, you can easily discern those whose faith discloses to them a reflection of the glory of Mary in you, from those who behold in you simply a daughter of Eve. Their conversation, deportment and looks, everything in them, will serve you as an index to this discernment. It is very difficult for man to disguise his real sentiments--dissimulation costs nature too dearly--but there are two circumstances wherein his moral character betrays itself in a striking manner, namely, in the presence of God, and in the presence of woman. It is neither permitted nor possible to a man truly religious and chaste to be bold or trivial in presence of either.

The woman illuminated by the sweet reflections of the glories of Mary, and imitating her virtues according to her state of life, enjoys the singular privilege of commanding the deferential respect of men of the most decided character. In her presence vice is silent, audacity is confounded, virtue, innocence and candor are at ease. The holy emanations of her heart purify the moral atmosphere around her, imparting to it a sweet and charming serenity, converting the place in which she appears into a kind of sanctuary.

By a contrary effect, resulting from a want of self-respect, woman becomes an easy prey to men of vain hearts and frivolous minds, who, not thinking themselves more obliged to respect her than she respects herself, without any reserve, give expression to the vanity of their hearts and thoughts. Everywhere and always ignorance or contempt of the Christian religion has begot contempt for woman, or disregard for her sacred rights and exalted dignity. Every where and always, irreligion has produced libertinism, the immediate and necessary effect of which is a depreciation of woman; and in those countries where the habits and institutions of the people have been deprived of the precious culture of Christianity, woman's condition is so abject that it differs in nothing from that of the brute, save that in *her* the sacred rights established by divine Providence are most shamefully violated.

That woman is worthy of glory or ignominy is the logical consequence of her being regarded as a daughter either of Eve or of Mary. In the one she is the poisoned source whence sin with all the evils that attend it flowed into the world, in the other she is the blessed source whence the Salvation of the world has issued forth. And, what she has been once for the entire human race in the garden of Eden and at Nazareth, she is yet every day for a people, a city, a family, or for each man in particular, according to the elevation of her position in society, and the extent of her influence.

The greater part of Christian nations owe to the prayers and examples of some holy woman, some pious queen, for instance, the gifts of Christianity and civilization--in this regard France has been, among all nations, singularly fortunate, and the name of Clotilda shall forever be revered in the pages of its history; while on the other hand, woman has often been instrumental in depriving the church of a kingdom, and in plunging into darkness and error a long succession of generations. For instances of this we have only to recall the names of Anne Boleyn and her cruel daughter, queen Elizabeth.

Countless numbers are indebted to woman for a knowledge of the truth, or the misfortune of forsaking it. Is there one who, in recalling the memories of the past, does not either bless or curse a woman, seeing in her an instrument of God's mercy, or of the seduction of Satan? Is there one who has not realized in that woman either a daughter of Eve or of the Blessed, Virgin--an Eden or a Nazareth? Behold the two poles between which the history of peoples and the life of each man in particular continually oscillate. Eve and Mary these are two guiding stars, either of which man must follow; the light of the one is deceitful and treacherous, while that of the other is true and beneficent; the one leads humanity along the paths of righteousness, while the other lures to the commission of sin. Hence it is that the church has given Mary those beautiful names, so significantly true: "Morning Star!" "Star of the Sea!"

This world is, indeed, like a stormy sea, in which are rocks and shoals, upon which man runs the risk of being wrecked unless he keeps his eyes steadfastly fixed upon this star whose brightness no storm can dim, and which, at the most perilous moment, shines with greater brilliancy, as the cheering sign of grace, hope and happiness. It is by turning our eyes toward Mary with her divine Son in her arms, presenting Him to us as our Saviour, that our troubled souls find the polar star which will quiet all their movements, and tranquilize the fluttering beatings of our troubled hearts. But, woe to us if, instead of fixing our attention upon Mary, virgin mother of God, we turn to Eve, infected with the contagion of the serpent, and offering to our hearts the doleful fruit of temptation and sin!

At the entrance to every path that leads to heaven or to the abyss of hell you will find a woman--the image of Mary, at the former, the image of Eve at the latter. It almost invariably happens that it is woman who deals out to mankind sin and death like Eve, or life, redemption and salvation like Mary. If you meet with one of these privileged men, chosen by God to be an instrument of His mercy, intimately associated with Jesus in the work of the salvation of His people, you may rest assured that this man owes to a woman, to a mother or a sister, the development of the great qualities which distinguish him. While, on the contrary, if you see one of those men tainted by the curse of some hereditary vice, very often more pernicious than original sin in its effects, you will discover that its source is the lesson or examples of a woman, whose poisoned influence shall oppress generations, just as that of Eve has oppressed the human race. Once again, I repeat it, that, as the corrupt and incredulous generation is the offspring of mothers modeled after Eve, so the holy and faithful generation traces its origin to mothers modeled after Mary.

You must choose between these two models, and on your choice will depend not only your own happiness and salvation, but also that of many yet unborn, whom God will confide to your care, and who will be dear to your heart. There remains no alternative; you will be either a cause of temptation and sin, or an instrument of grace and benediction for those who will live with you. You will either offer them the forbidden fruit like your mother Eve, or you will give spiritual birth to the Word of Life for them. As one of the greatest torments of the reprobate woman in hell will be to see the woeful misery into which she has brought those whom she had loved so dearly upon earth, and to hear the maledictions and reproaches which they shall hurl against her, so, also, one of the greatest joys of the faithful woman in heaven, will be to see those whom she sanctified by word and example now grouped around her, crowning her with a diadem of glory as a mark of everlasting gratitude.

Would you deprive your soul of this saintly joy, and condemn it to suffer the punishment reserved for those women who will be the cause of the ruin and eternal perdition of many? Divine justice shall vindicate itself, even in this life, by making your heart a most cruel torment to itself, that you may expiate, in agonizing torture your infidelity to grace. The cause of your sin shall be the very means of your punishment. God will employ, to avenge His outraged honor and His violated laws, those whom you have turned away from Him, and who, recognizing in you the cause of their evils, will end, perhaps, by hating you, or, what is still worse, by despising you. Oh, may it never be your sad fate to feel the withering contempt of those who have been led away from God by your bad or undue influence, that is, by loving them for *yourself* and not for *God and themselves*! Do not, I pray you, store up such bitterness for your old age, such anguish for your death-bed, since, instead of bitter regrets, you can experience a sweet joy, which is a foretaste of never-ending happiness, a special consolation for God's faithful friends at that last and dreadful moment when the soul stands trembling on the threshold of eternity; may it be your envied privilege to leave after you upon earth souls edified by your example, and grateful for the good you have done them.

CHAPTER VI.
EVE AND MARY CONTINUED.

The history of the fall of man, caused by Eve, and of his restoration, brought about by Mary, is a subject of grave consideration for women of serious minds, for women who have at heart the preservation of the dignity and vocation of their sex. By a close consideration of these two models, which furnish the solution to so many enigmas, explaining so many truths and throwing so much light upon the most obscure and the most profound questions, they will learn by a short and easy method what they should do, and what they should avoid; they will learn how sin has been propagated, the reason why it still exists; they will learn how justice and virtue flourish upon earth, how men turn away from God, and how they return to Him. It was with reason that God allowed sin and justice to attain us through the agency of woman, and that her free consent was a necessary condition for both the ruin and the restoration of the human race.

It is therefore an interesting and useful study to consider in their detail and most minute circumstances the acts (so extremely opposed) of these two women, for one of them, according to the beautiful expression of the Church, has restored to us by her divine Son what the other had deprived us of by her disobedience. There is in these two facts, so different in their nature and results, a wonderful gradation which points out to us the fatal declivity by which the human heart insensibly sinks to the lowest abyss of evil, or rises to the highest degree of virtue and glory. In the sin of Eve the first degree was a certain intemperance of language, which led her to reply to the insidious questions of the devil; in appearance this forgetfulness was very slight. To answer a question, give an explanation requested of you, clear up a doubt, render an account of a precept of the Lord, seem at first sight something natural and permitted. It is quite easy to be deceived in this matter. We readily convince ourselves that we are actuated by laudable motives in such like conversations--motives for gloryfying God and justifying His providence; but we should be extremely cautious: language is something august and sacred, for it is the tie that unites the soul to God, and man to his fellow-men,--it is the mysterious knot of all societies, divine and human.

Language establishes between those who speak a more intimate relation than they are generally aware of. Few persons realize the prodigious transfusion of thoughts, sentiments, influence and life that arise from conversation. Have you clearly understood this truth in its full force? Language establishes between souls a very close and mysterious union, and this is why discretion, prudence and reserve are so necessary in regulating its use. This is why Jesus Christ warns us in the Gospel, that we shall render an account of *every idle word*, if indeed we may call idle a thing that entails such frightful consequences or fatal results.

If this reserve is necessary for all it is more especially so for woman, who, being more communicative than man, experiences a greater necessity to speak--to express herself more freely, and in terms more explicit. If women were sincere and impartial judges of themselves they for the most part would not fail to recognize that nearly all their faults spring from a useless word--an imprudent answer, or an indiscreet question.

The word why is indeed very short, but in its insidious brevity it comprises a multitude of things which are all the more dangerous because they are unforeseen, being concealed in a perfidious and cloudy vagueness. Why? This word is the beginning of the greater part of those temptations against frailty. The enemy, seeking our destruction, almost invariably announces his presence by this captious question, either by the mouth of another or by our own mind, in order to fill the heart with doubt and trouble. Why take such and such precautions? Why avoid such a place, such a person, such company? Why renounce such and such amusements? Why neglect or cast off that ornament? Why suffer this or that privation? Why abstain from this action, which is not bad in itself? Why turn away the ear from those praises, those compliments, dictated by usage or etiquette, to keep up that intercourse without which society would be impossible? Why not read this book, this novel? Why not assist at this play which the most rigorous moralist would not condemn; and which has for its object to inspire horror for vice, by placing before our eyes its doleful consequences true to reality? Why restrain to inaction the finest faculties of the soul, and refuse them the aliment they so ardently crave? Why deprive our heart and imagination of the pleasures which the beautiful inspires? Why not form at an early age a taste for worldly beauty, and be possessed of all the resources and advantages that it affords us during life? Why be mistrustful of the mind and heart, at an age when they still possess all their simplicity and freshness, through vain fear which renders after-life almost intolerable? Why not be more confiding in the heart's fidelity and in the goodness of God, who has not condemned man to constant privations?--Such is the language that the enemy of our eternal salvation and happiness addresses us every day with such perfidious adroitness; and who, spite of the experience of those whom he has already deceived, deceives us every day.

This language is the more perfidious for being apparently truthful and natural. When there is question of corrupting a heart that is yet virtuous, vice conceals itself under the mantle of virtue, as otherwise its efforts would be powerless. Now, we can safely say that its venom has already tainted the young lady's heart, when, through inattention and want of vigilance, she has suffered doubt to brood over any of those obligations which are so delicate and difficult to determine, and, nevertheless, most grave and important, since they entail, when neglected, the most disastrous results. Firmness of mind, assurance in her convictions, a clear and strong consciousness of duty, are to her indispensable qualifications; and when she suffers this tenor of conduct to be interfered with by imprudently replying, like Eve, to a captious question, the peace and innocence of her heart are certainly threatened.

The young girl's innocence is something that is very imperfectly known; the delicate and almost imperceptible shades that reflect its beauty and which render it delightful to God and His angels, escape the general notice of mankind. It is composed of a chaste ignorance of mind, a great simplicity of heart, and a constant and unwavering firmness of will. Now, what merits our greatest attention is the fact that this firmness of will begins to give way in woman the moment she removes, even by a slight doubt, this precious veil of ignorance which protects her virtue, or when, by an indiscreet question, or an imprudent answer, she exposes the simplicity of her heart.

The virtues which adorn the heart of a young lady are concealed from her own knowledge. God has so enveloped her in mystery that He alone understands her.

None other save the penetrating eye of God should look into the sanctuary of her heart. None other than His light should shine in this holy and chaste obscurity, and this is why humility, of which we have found so perfect a model in Mary, should be the necessary shield and guarantee of a young lady's innocence. She ought not to have the slightest misgivings relative to the value of the treasure she possesses or the loss she would sustain in losing it.

The presence of an angel sufficed to trouble Mary. Oh, young ladies should meditate well and frequently on the conduct that Mary observed in this interview, and imitate her example! She did not answer the Angel's words, but she observed an humble and modest silence. Not so with Eve who, without reflection, answered the devil's question, and by this first reply began a conversation the issue of which has proved so disastrous to the whole human race. Learn from this two-fold example, and from the effects so different which have resulted from both, how much you should fear Eve's curiosity in yourself, and with what care and assiduity you should labor to imitate the reserve and silence of Mary.

Curiosity is a most dangerous rock for a young lady,--this is the rock upon which a countless number of your sex and age have been wrecked. The moment that you pander to the desire of knowing everything, you immediately enter on a most dangerous way, the issue of which is at least precarious. It was for having satisfied this desire that Eve opened the door to all the calamities that afflict and will afflict mankind till the end of time. And, since then, it has caused the ruin of a countless number of women.

Intrench, so to speak, your mind in the citadel of your own heart. Let it repose in the holy obscurity of an humble and docile faith, and you will learn more useful things in this way than you could ever learn even from the best books and the most eloquent instructions. Faith and prayer should be the daily food of your soul. Faith, with its imperfect yet celestial light, will meet all the legitimate wants of your mind; and prayer, with its divine unction, will embalm your soul.

Often turn your eyes toward heaven, and earth will soon lose all its attractions. Converse frequently with God and you will find it easier to dispense with the intercourse of men; keep your mind at a remote distance from all worldly knowledge, and the innocence of your heart will enjoy sweet repose. Seek not to anticipate by an indiscreet precipitancy the time when the realities of life shall open out to your view. Perhaps, more than once you will regret the happiness which you now enjoy, and which is due both to your knowledge and ignorance of things.

In reality, you possess by faith the same knowledge that the blessed have in heaven, that knowledge which has been the object of the study, research and love of the most renowned minds and of the most perfect souls in this world. Faith, elevating you above yourself and all earthly things, leads you to regions to which the most distinguished genius, joined to the most profound and persevering study, can never approach. Faith makes you in a certain way the sister of angels and of men,-- of men who have been the most remarkable on earth for their excellent qualities of head and heart. Faith associates you with the glorious choirs of heaven, and, when truly lively and active, will bring you unalloyed felicity and ineffable joy.

Why should you envy those women, who, for being older than you, have gained by experience a knowledge of things that you should still ignore? Why seek to compare their knowledge with that which you possess? The knowledge that you have obtained by faith has cost your mind no effort--not a single regret to your heart, no remorse to your conscience. Every step that you make in this illuminated way recalls to your mind a sweet and precious souvenir, the pure reflections of which will be the only light that will dispel the gloom of the trials and anguish of life. It shall be very different with regard to what you must learn in time to come. Experience is a severe teacher, whose lessons are dearly bought; this is clearly and forcibly expressed by the Holy Ghost saying: "He that adds something to the knowledge already acquired, adds at the same time new pains to those he already suffers."

So far you have learned the one thing necessary to man, and which meets all his wants: you have learned how to please God, to love and serve Him by the observance of His commandments, and fidelity to his inspirations, acknowledging and honoring His authority and power over you in your parents, who are, in your regard, His representatives. So that at present duty possessing pleasing attractions offers none of those difficulties which, at a later period of life, will render it often-times painful. Your virtues, protected by that reserve which the world itself has imposed upon youth, guarded by the vigilance of a tender and careful mother, aided by her examples, encouraged by her exhortations and love, tranquilly grow up in the modest sanctuary of the family, without the remotest idea of the trials they must one day meet with.

To learn what pertains to faith and salvation, good will suffices. We are always sure to succeed in pleasing God when we are sincerely desirous to serve Him; in this regard we can never anticipate Him. Not so with the science which teaches how to please men and secure their good will or favor, to enter into their views, conform to their laws and customs. No matter how great our desire may be to succeed, we are never sure of success, and very often the efforts made to secure it remove us farther from the desired end. Consequently, very often the surest means of securing the esteem of the world is to despise it, and withdraw from its tyranny. If you fail to disengage yourself from it, and if you wish to servilely adhere to its maxims, you will often experience that they are severe and hard; and you will reproach yourself more than once for having desired in your youth to taste of those fruits, externally so beautiful but internally so bitter.

Hence, moderation of the mind's curiosity is necessary, and in order to satisfy its activity apply it to those things that can be of interest to your conscience and salvation, to the knowledge and study of those sublime truths which, while enlightening your intelligence, will elevate your heart and strengthen your will. The knowledge that you will acquire in this way will serve you for the rest of your life, much more than all the profane and useless books that you can read. Accustom your mind to the love and search of serious things; this will prove to be of invaluable utility to you. There is little consistency in frivolous things, and those, who have fed their souls upon them during youth, find themselves void and abandoned when they arrive at the age when woman can please only by interesting the mind and heart by solid charms and tried virtue. This is the age which you should constantly keep before your mind, because it is the one that lasts the longest, and which disposes us proximately for that awful moment in which our fate will be decided forever. Endeavor to become at an early age what you should be during the greater part of your life, and what you would desire to have been at the hour of death.

CHAPTER VII.
THE WORLD.

The world is like some objects which, when seen from afar, deceive the eyes and allure the imagination; but on approaching or touching them their charms vanish. It is like those carcasses that retain the form of a human body as long as they are buried in the obscurity of the tomb, but which, on being exposed to the air, are immediately reduced to dust. Those who are separated from it without having ever known it are exposed to be deceived by its perfidious allurements; and those who, in order to know it, with a view of despising it, desire to mingle in its feasts and pleasures, run a greater danger of falling a victim to the seductions and corruption of its charms.-- How, then, shall you secure the advantage and escape the danger?

By shunning the world, you secure your heart and conscience against its seductions; but this evasion, leaving you to consider it from a remote standpoint exposes your mind to prejudices favorable to it, and which, later, might become for you the source of many errors and of many faults. How shall you surmount this twofold difficulty? On the one hand you cannot mingle with the world without danger, and on the other hand it will not do for you to ignore its dangers which must be known in order to be avoided. This dilemma would be of no consequence to a frivolous and unreflecting soul, or to a vain and presumptuous mind, which, confiding in its own powers, believes that it has a good knowledge only of what it sees and experiences; and counts for naught the teachings of faith and the experience of those who have gone before.

Let not this be your case, but, listening with an humble and docile heart to the teachings of faith, reason and experience, learn to know the world and its dangers while your age and condition still shield you from its seductions. Of all the means by which divine Providence enlightens our minds here below, divine faith, as you are aware, is the purest, the brightest and the most reliable,--not only because it comes from God, but because it is presented to us by an authority which He has established, and which, by His special assistance, He preserves from all error.

Sacred Scripture, interpreted and explained to you by this authority is, therefore, the great source to which you must have recourse for the knowledge of the things you *should* know. Now you will find that there is hardly a single page of those sacred writings in which there is not a malediction pronounced against the world, and a warning for you to avoid its siren charms. You will find in the gospel according to St. John its true character described by Jesus Christ Himself, who, being the Incarnate Wisdom, could not have any other than the most perfect idea of things according to their just value.

In the first place, it is certain, according to this Apostle, that when the Eternal Word came into the world it knew Him not; when Jesus wished to make the Jews feel the confusion of their own blindness, and see the reason of their opposition to His doctrine, He said: You are from beneath, I am from above, you are of this world, I am not of this world, therefore, I say to you that you shall die in your sins. (John viii. 23, 24.) Could there be anything more explicit in condemnation of the world? It has its origin and the throne of its power in the lower regions of the earth, while the kingdom of God resides in the sublime abode of the human heart.

When He promised His disciples that He would send them the Spirit of Truth, to console them, He gave as the distinctive mark by which they would know the Holy Spirit, that the world could not receive Him because it has no knowledge of Him. Hence the opposition that exists between the world and the spirit of the New Law is so great that any compromise is impossible. The world is absolutely incompetent to receive or understand the spirit of Jesus Christ. Another fact will render this manifest opposition still more palpable. When Jesus addressed His eternal Father that beautiful prayer preceding His agony and passion, He excluded the world by a positive act of His will, in order to give all to understand that the world could never have any share with Him. "*I pray not for the world but for them whom thou hast given me. The world hath hated them because they are not of the world as I also am not of the world.*" (John xvii. 9, 14.)

St. Paul interprets these words in that energetic style so characteristic of his writings, when he says to the Corinthians that "we have not received the spirit of this world whose wisdom is folly before God." Now shall you adopt as the rule of your conduct and judgment a wisdom which God has not only reproved, but even branded with the stigma of folly? According to the same Apostle the world proves by its own words that its knowledge is stupidity, since it can see nothing but folly in the cross. The maxims, ideas, judgments, conduct and habits of the world and those of the flock that Jesus came to save are so contradictory, their language is so different, that the wise of the one are fools with the other; and the things regarded as the most sublime by the former are to the latter preposterous absurdities. The reason is simply because the one has its origin, light and end in heaven, while the other draws them from the earth.

Now, if, in order to verify these words of the Sacred Scriptures, you take a view of the doctrine of the world and of that of Jesus Christ, and compare them, you will not find a single point in the one that is not in direct contradiction to the other; so that, by the Gospel, you are enabled to discover the maxims of the world, and *vice versa*. You may rest assured that what is recommended and sought for by the one is censured and despised by the other. St. Paul, speaking to the Galatians, says; that "if he was still pleasing to men he would not be the servant of Jesus Christ."

If this be the case, you will say, why remain in the world? Is it not every one's duty to leave it as soon as possible and abandon it to its own corruption? Let the words of our divine Lord answer: "*I do not pray you to remove them from the world, but I pray you to preserve them from evil.*" Our peace of conscience in this life, and the joys of heaven hereafter require separation from the world and opposition to its maxims. But this separation is one of mind and heart, which consists in a manner of thinking, judging and acting entirely opposed to that of the world. Man ceases to belong to the world the moment he has ceased to make it the arbitrator of his conduct and judgment, and when he has freed himself from its prejudices, caprices and tyranny. Behold what religion requires of you, and what alone will insure you happiness in this life and in the next.

Now, what is this world from which we must separate in order to lead a Christian life? In any society, that we wish to study with a view to obtain a knowledge of its nature and objects, we may consider either the laws by which it is governed, or the body of men who compose it and who are governed by these laws.

Considered from the first point of view, the world consists in its own maxims, laws, customs and judgments, which are in opposition to the letter and spirit of the Gospel; and which tend to withdraw the soul from the love of spiritual things, or at least to create in her a dislike for them.

Considered from the second point of view, the world comprises a mass of men who profess its maxims, adopt its usages, obey its laws, and yield to its judgments.

The world thus considered entails a twofold obligation for you, one of which can never admit of any exception or dispensation, while the observance of the other must be always regulated by prudence and charity. Indeed the world, considered in its maxims, should be for you an object of constant aversion and contempt, because it is the arch enemy of Jesus Christ and of the spirit that He communicates to His true disciples. This is the world that you renounced on the day of your baptism; and the solemn engagement that you then made was the first and most important of all those that you have made, or will make, during life.

But, while it is never permitted you to adopt the maxims of the world, charity, prudence, and the consideration due to your position, age and family, will not allow you to effectively isolate yourself from those who have adopted its maxims as the rule of their actions and judgments. In this you should conform to all that due decorum requires, and endeavor to preserve your mind and heart against the pernicious influences often communicated by words, actions, lessons or examples of those who are slaves of the laws or customs of the world. The danger is the more imminent inasmuch as the sunny side only of the world is displayed to you; while no pains are spared on the part of those bound to you by the most sacred ties to engage you to adopt their views and imitate their example. This is certainly one of the most delicate positions in which a young lady can be placed, when her only arms of defense are the uprightness of her mind, the innocence of her heart and the purity of her instincts.

St. Bernard says, "to serve God is to reign." By a contradictory assertion, we can safely say, to serve the world is to be a slave; and of all servitudes there is none so hard nor so humiliating as that which the world imposes upon those who yield to its empire. If God were so exacting as the world, so inflexible in the laws that He imposes upon us, so severe in the chastisements by which delinquencies are punished, piety would be an insupportable burden through the weakness of the greater part of men; and God would find very few worshipers who would be willing to submit to such an ordeal.

What is most remarkable and worthy of compassion is the fact that, very often, those who groan the most under this slavery are at the same time those who support it with the greatest resignation.

To suffer for a genuine duty, for a generous sentiment, for a noble or grand idea, is something which the human heart can, not only accept, but even love and choose with a certain pride; but to suffer for the sake of worldly etiquette, for the sake of fashion, for things and parsons despised for their tyranny, is a deplorable humiliation for those who do it. And, nevertheless, the greater part of those who might be called world-worshipers, who seem to give it the *tone*, bear patiently its yoke, which debases them in their own eyes,--pandering to necessities which they have imprudently created, and from which they now find it impossible to free themselves.

CHAPTER VIII.
THE SAME SUBJECT CONTINUED.

IF the life of a woman of the world were proposed as a model, and, after having carefully examined all her occupations, you would discover what would be hard for you to be convinced of before having done so, namely: that there are women so inconsiderate as to feast their minds on such frivolities, so forgetful of their dignity as to make it subservient to such misery, so trifling as to make a serious work of *bag itelles*, which at most can be considered as little better than childish amusement; your soul, still rich in its primitive candor, and favored with an energy tempered in the love and habit of virtue, would revolt at the thought of such debasement. And, nevertheless, unless you apply your mind to acquire a love for serious matters you will not escape a disorder which you so justly deplore in others; you will be captured in those windings which have proved fatal fastnesses to women of other days. There remains no choice between these two alternatives: you must either found your conduct upon intelligence enlightened by faith, or abandon it, like a rudderless ship, to the caprice of passion and pleasure.

The life of a worldly woman is a fictitious life: nature seems to have no attractions for her; her soul has lost all taste for its charms; she studiously endeavors to shut out its influences, and to subvert as much as possible the order by which it is governed. This estrangement, this disgust with nature, haunts her wherever she goes, even in the making of her toilet, even in the employment of her time. She converts day into night and night into day, giving to pleasure the time destined for repose; she purloins from the industrious hours of day the sleep and rest for which her wearied limbs and excited imagination contend.

While she is sleeping, the humble daughter of St. Benedict or St. Dominic leaves her cell to sing the praises of the Lord, and offer Him the day with its duties consecrated without reserve to His glory. When heavy curtains screen her restless slumber from the sun's obtrusive light, the pious daughter of St. Vincent de Paul descends into the folds of her own heart in meditation, and enkindles in the fire of divine love the charity with which she must cheer the poor or sick whom she is destined to visit during the day.

What a difference between those two lives! The worldling rises rested, but not from a refreshing sleep, she is aroused perhaps by the importunate rays of the mid-day sun or by the noisy tramping of hardy workmen who, after their half day's work is done, return home to partake of a frugal repast and receive the sweet greetings of a Christian family. It is then that her day begins, as also the series of the *grave* occupations that are destined to fill it. The time is short and scarcely suffices to prepare herself for the evening amusements; all her energies are now employed to give herself that external grace and charm necessary to render her conspicuous in the joyous circle. Alas! the worldly woman is entirely absorbed in herself, and when she does something for others, it is with a view to secure her own interest or pleasure. That devotedness, that generous sacrifice and disinterestedness characteristic of true friendship is to her a mere paradox, as she is an entire stranger to its effects and charms.

After her toilet, her most serious occupations are the visits which she pays and receives. A visit prompted by charity or some other virtue is good, highly commendable and praiseworthy. I admire and understand the woman who leaves the peaceful company of her family, when no pressing need requires her presence, to go and visit the poor and destitute, in order to sweeten their bitter lot by a word of encouragement or a little alms. I understand and admire her who readily sacrifices her legitimate joy in order to go and mingle her tears with those of her friend and mitigate her sorrow or share it with her. I understand and esteem the woman who, impressed by the superior wisdom and exemplary piety of another woman, goes to her for advice, devoting with pleasure her leisure hours to that end. I see in all these circumstances a motive that is serious, honorable, praiseworthy, and capable of acting upon a noble heart and an elevated intelligence. But, among the visits made by worldly women; how few there are that are prompted by such motives! The greater part of those women visit with no other view than to pass the time, to pander to their own vanity and curiosity, to form or execute some intrigue. What is said and done in their visits is worthy of the motive that inspires them. There is not a single serious thought expressed, not a single word to show that these women have an intelligence capable of comprehending the truth, a heart made to love what is good, or a soul capable of receiving God Himself. If life were but a dream, if there be no hereafter, if at death the soul must perish with the body; and man must sink into the nothingness whence he sprang; they would have nothing to change in their visits, conversations and conduct.

There is a visit celebrated in Holy Writ, a visit paid by a young woman to one of her own sex but more advanced in years, a visit so holy and renowned that its anniversary is celebrated throughout the Christian world,--it is the visit paid by the Blessed Virgin to her cousin St. Elizabeth. O, Christian ladies, behold your true model! Compare this visit with yours, and judge yourselves according to it. Compare your motives with those of Mary. Compare your conversations with that sublime conversation of which the sacred writer has given us a fragment, being the most sublime canticle that has ever been uttered by any intelligent creature under the action of divine inspiration. Oh, what a world-wide difference between this sublime canticle and the light and frivolous conversations in which so many women indulge; if you were to look for the reverse of this heavenly visit you would invariably find it among the visits paid by worldly women.

Mary carries with her the Son of God, the Author of grace, the Principle of eternal life, the Source of chaste desires and holy hopes. The worldly woman carries with her in her visits the spirit of the world, the spirit of deception, egotism and folly, which is in every way opposed to the spirit of Christianity. Mary sings the praises of humility and proclaims it the virtue beloved of God,--the virtue which secures His love and assistance; she extols the happiness of those who thirst for justice and truth, deploring at the same time the spiritual poverty and indigence of those who are puffed up with self-conceit. The worldly woman, on the contrary, seeks in her conversations to flatter her vanity and pride by parading the empty resources of her imagination and misguided intelligence. She envies the happiness of those who, rich in beauty and all those qualities that charm, draw many admirers around them. Elizabeth, on beholding her cousin, felt her infant leap for joy. The worldly woman stirs up in the hearts of those whom she visits the most frivolous instincts, and sometimes even the worst passions.

This tableau excites your love and disgust. The comparison frightens you; and perhaps in the simplicity of your heart you will say, it is not free from exaggeration. On the contrary, you will be sadly disappointed when, at a more advanced age, you will clearly see that this is a very mild and subdued picture of what is true and real. Your age and innocence do not allow me to reveal to you all the mysteries of sin--all the snares, all the dangers, all the frivolities that fill up the days of a worldly woman.

Would that what I have said of her may inspire you with salutary horror for her life; and make you shun the snares in which she has been taken! I pray that you, satisfied with the knowledge you have of her follies, may never feel the desire of adding to what you already know, the fatal knowledge imparted by experience! That you may never forget these words of St. John: *Love not the world, nor the things which are in the world; for all that is in the world is the concupiscence of the flesh and the concupiscence of the eyes and the pride of life.* (I John ii. 15-16.)

CHAPTER IX.
THE WILL.

S t. John, the Apostle, addressing those who have not yet passed the age of adolescence, says in his first Epistles: *"I write unto you, because ... you have overcome the wicked one."* Then speaking to those who have attained the age of manhood, he says: *"I write to you, young men, because you are strong, and the word of God abideth in you, and you have overcome the wicked one."* Again, in the book of Proverbs, chapter xxxi, the inspired writer speaks in the following terms: *"who shall find a valiant woman? The price of her is as of things brought from afar off, and from the uttermost coasts ... She hath put out her hand to strong things ... strength and beauty are her clothing; and she shall laugh in the latter day, she hath opened her mouth to wisdom and the law of clemency is on her tongue.... Favor is deceitful, and beauty is vain; the woman that feareth the Lord, she shall be praised. Give her of the fruit of her hands; and let her works praise her in the gates."*

Thus, according to Holy Writ, fortitude or strength is the portion of youth, which is manifested by the victories of the will over the enemy of our salvation. This valor is regarded by the sacred writer as one of the finest qualities with which woman can be adorned, since she owes to it all her true success and glory. Now what is this precious quality? In what faculty of the soul does it reside? What are the signs by which its presence is made manifest? What is the end to which it tends? What are the rewards that crown its victories? These are questions of deep interest, and the importance attached to a knowledge of their solution cannot be too great.

In the first place we shall begin by stating that the seat of valor is found in the will. To be valiant consists in willing intensely what is painful to nature, accomplishing what is proposed with energy and perseverance. I have often treated this subject, but it is so inexhaustible that it always seems new. Its importance grows with time, and now-a-days it cannot be insisted on too much, nor can there be too much attention paid to it by those who wish to preserve in this world the integrity of their conscience and lead an irreproachable life.

Alas it is painful to avow that this generous will is too rarely met with. This noble faculty of the soul is made subservient to other faculties which should be subject to and directed by it. The mind has perhaps acquired greater vivacity and penetration. The imagination, under the action of a constant change of images, and those sensations which the activity of life multiplies so rapidly in our time, has perhaps become richer and more varied. The heart, cherished while young by the cares and caresses common to the paternal roof, has perhaps more confidence and candor. But the will, what has become of it, what has it gained by this development of all the powers of the soul? Where is its place among them? It should be their ruler, whereas it is made their slave; they have conspired its overthrow.

It is true that very often the enfeebling of this great faculty is due to the excessive tenderness of those who have allowed us to contract pernicious habits. Who is it that speaks to the child's will? Who teaches him how to use that faculty and resist with energy the caprices of his imagination, the passions of the heart, the empire of the senses, the seductions of the world? These are duties that the will is called on to discharge, and as long as man shall live such duties will be of daily occurrence,-- hence the will is destined to be constantly called into action.

The will serves us when all the other faculties fail to act. When the exhausted imagination sinks into a lethargic slumber; when the worried heart loses all relish for everything; when the mind, dreading the light of truth, gives itself over to error and prejudice; when the smoke of passion blinds the intelligence and suffocates the senses; it is then that the will, fashioned in the school of pliant energy, seizing the reins with a firm and vigorous grasp, snatches the imagination from its torpor by bringing it to bear on objects capable of arousing it; it is then that the will animates the heart with generous and noble sentiments, and applies the mind to the consideration of truths which enlighten and fortify it.

There exists a strange abuse relative to the nature and essence of the will. Very often, parents, blinded by a false prejudice, see with pleasure, and admire in their children, stubbornness and obstinacy of character; and, looking forward to their future with an air of pride, they say: "That child will have a strong will." Deplorable error! Woe to the parents who fall into it, and the children who are its object! When the will is truly strong, far from being obstinate it is, on the contrary, pliant and tractable. No human power can restore suppleness to the arm which a convulsive paroxysm has stiffened, yet it does not follow that this arm is stronger than when it was in a healthy condition. The stiffness, far from increasing its strength, decidedly weakens it. In like manner the will's strength does not lie in stubborn obstinacy, but rather in that pliancy which enables it to dispose itself as circumstances may require.

A stubborn character has nothing in common with this noble and precious faculty of the soul. And, like all the others, this faculty possesses two degrees of elevation; in the one it comes in direct contact with the senses and, the external world; and in the other, raised above all sensibility, it receives its light and movement from on high.

The will, taken in its inferior part, is nothing else than that appetite or blind instinct which we hold in common with the brute creation; and by which animals are governed in their choice of some things and their rejection of others. If the will, properly so called, consisted in this blind instinct, man would be inferior to the ass and the mule, whose attractions and repugnances are more imperious than those of other animals. The will, as understood in the true Christian sense of the term, acts in contradiction to this brutal appetite; hence they alone have a strong will who can, when duty and conscience require it, obey their voice with docility, in spite of all instinctive opposition.

The education of the will, I admit, is a long and painful process. We are taught at a dear rate how to *know* and *judge* things; but we must learn at a dearer price how to *will*. The culture of the mind is the least important and the easiest part of our education, while the culture of the will is extremely important and demands much time and labor; yet, through a most culpable negligence, it is just the faculty that receives the least attention and culture. Too many imagine that the training of the will may be done at any time and, what is still more erroneous, that age, experience and events will suffice to do this work. Hence we see every day poor souls entering the scene of life without an educated will, which alone is capable of reacting against the evils and trials from which none in this world can escape. This is the cause of that imbecility which renders the most precious qualities of mind and heart useless; generating inconsistencies and uncertainties which, in the moment of trial, deprive the heart of its energy and the mind of all light, thus leaving the soul open to all the assaults of misfortune.

We are obliged to chronicle a painful truth when we assert that the culture of the will is sadly neglected in education in general, but more especially so in that of women. There are even some so blind as to think that a strong will in woman is a dangerous quality, alleging, as a proof of their assertion, the puerile reason, that since woman was made to obey she should find in another's will the rule of her actions. But, we ask, if woman can have no will of her own, how can she exercise the virtue of obedience, since that virtue consists in bending the will to duty? And since, in her sphere, she is constantly called on to practice obedience it is just the reason why she should have a strong will.

Now if from a tender age she has not given due attention to this precious faculty of her soul; if she has contracted the fatal habit of acting without a purpose, without reflecting, through caprice, following by a blind instinct the allurements that flatter the senses and imagination; if she has not learned to conquer herself, to put duty before pleasure, and the voice of conscience above that of the passions and honor; how will she be able to live with a husband capricious perhaps in his desires and stubborn in his will? How will she be able to confront his exactions or cope with his rage? How will she bear with the faults of her servants and of those with whom she may be obliged to live? How will she, in her warnings and reproaches be able to blend in a just proportion mildness and firmness, to obtain the salutary effects which she desires?

The path of life is not strewn with flowers; all is not joy and happiness here below. Woman is destined, as well as man, to meet with days of sorrow and bitterness, when a firm, patient will must be her only port of safety. To woman patience is, perhaps of all virtues, the most necessary to sustain her in mental anxieties and various other sufferings that are inevitable; and, since patience is a fruit of the will, it follows that a morbid will cannot produce an enduring patience, the deficiency of which must render her life almost intolerable.

He that sails with the current and a favorable wind need not ply his oars; but when there is question of going in the contrary direction, what was at first a great advantage becomes now a double disadvantage, and he can succeed only by strenuous efforts.

During the days of youthful glee you glide gaily down the river of life, going with the current, favored by the breeze of hope, charmed by varied and softly-changing scenes. But this time will soon have an end: sorrow will embitter your joys ere the frost of age shall have cooled the blood or chilled the imagination; very soon, in a few years, perhaps, it will knock at the door of your soul; and you will be obliged to give this inopportune visitor admittance, to remain with you, perhaps, for the rest of your life. Among the young ladies of your acquaintance are there not some who are unhappy? And can you, without a voluntary illusion, convince yourself that youth is a preservative against misfortune? Are you prepared to ward off the intruder? If it wounds you how will you endure the pain? It is imprudent to delay the acquisition of a particular branch of learning until its practical use becomes necessary; and since it is while we are hale and hearty that we should learn to die well, so it is while prosperity smiles on us that we should learn to bear adversity. Learn now, while young, to support all the vicissitudes of life; make timely provision, not only against adversity, but also against prosperity, which for many is the more dangerous of the two.

Prepare to meet not only those who will try your patience by their unjust or troublesome doings, but also those whose affection officiousness, and flattery, will perhaps exact from you a greater exercise of virtue. Be on your guard, not only against others, but also against yourself. Learn to bear with yourself, to suffer with courage the inconstancy of your own humor, the nights of your imagination, the impetuosity of your character, the violent and inordinate movements of your heart. Accustom your will to wield the scepter and resolutely to govern the passions, which are most powerful auxiliaries for good or for evil,--for good when under the complete control of the will, for evil when they are emancipated from its sway, for then they become the vultures of life, and a torment of the soul.

Never lose sight of the fact that you require a stronger will to obey than to command, and that your condition, far from rendering your will less necessary, shows, on the contrary, that it is indispensable to you; unless, by indorsing that unjust and outrageous judgment by which the world seeks to degrade the dignity of woman, you force upon yourself the conviction that her will should count for nothing either at home or abroad,--that she is destined to be blindly led by the caprices of others; unless you confound obedience with servitude, and authorize the prejudices of those who pretend that woman should have neither thought nor will of her own, but that another is charged with thinking and willing for her, thus exonerating her from all responsibility.

If this be your conviction, I ask: "Why do you read this book? Close it, it is not written for you; because from the first page to the last it constantly discloses to your view all the titles of your glory and the grandeur of your dignity. Close your eyes to the light of truth, shackle the will's liberty lest you may see and feel the shame and humiliation of your sad condition; and, like a thing inert, await in dumb silence until some trafficker may come and calculate how much he will gain in fortune and pleasure by purchasing you!" Behold the deplorable condition to which the pagan theories of the world reduce woman! behold the degree of abjection to which she herself descends when, losing sight of the light of faith, which exposes the true nature of things, she suffers herself to be deceived by the vain systems of a world worthy of God's anathemas, and governed by the spirit of deception.

No, woman has not been created to be a slave; God has neither destined nor consigned to such a humiliating state that half of humanity from which He has chosen His mother, and which has been favored with a holy reflection of the glory of Mary. God required a positive act of woman's will in her co-operation in the work of our redemption,--and to obtain it He did not hesitate to choose as His ambassador, one of the brightest of His archangels. Judge from this the respect and importance due to woman's will. Moreover, it is a significant truth, sustained by a long experience, that the salvation of a family, of a father, a brother, a son, a husband, is secured in a great measure by the care and prayers, the firm and wise, yet mild and prudent conduct of a Christian woman, deeply penetrated with the profound sentiment of her dignity and the true importance of her duties,--all of which depend upon a firm and patient will.

CHAPTER X.
THE IMAGINATION.

The imagination, that active agent of the senses, is the bee which, in its continual excursions, gathers from the flower-cups the sweet scented dust from which, by due process, it forms the wax that gives us light and the honey that nourishes us. Your soul is like a bee-hive, full of activity and life. The external world is like a flower-garden, in which each flower has its peculiar color, perfume and brightness. Your imagination is the working bee of this hive, which resounds with the humming of the senses. The will governs and directs all with perfect harmony, when peaceful order reigns in all its workings. But the moment that the will fails to discharge the duties of its office, the imagination and the senses, like bees deprived of their queen, wander hither and thither without any determined purpose, and the hive is abandoned to inaction or disorder.

It is of paramount importance to you to have a clear knowledge of the nature, end and functions of all the faculties of your soul; so that you may keep them within the province that God has allotted to them, and that no disorder may arise from the attempted encroachments of some upon others. This point becomes one of grave importance when there is question of *the imagination*, because it is the most rash, most ambitious, most violent and at the same time, the most seductive, of all the faculties.

Holding an intermediate place between the soul and the senses, it is the most accessible to the charms of the external world, and participates in the inconstant and tumultuous movements of our own sensibility. Confined to its own sphere of action, it is a precious auxiliary, which often facilitates the perception of the truth, and the accomplishment of good, by presenting them to the mind and heart under colors that render them amiable and attractive. When properly employed, it is an invaluable gift of God, who has given it to us to aid the infirmity of our nature, by rendering less painful the efforts that we are so often obliged to make in order to triumph over our bad inclinations. But when we fail to make a proper use of it, it then becomes for us a source of danger, and a great obstacle to our advancement towards perfection.

Placed between the will and the senses, it should neither be controlled by the latter nor emancipated from the sway of the former. The faithful observance of this condition can alone insure us all the advantages we may hope to derive from it. Should it prove to be a frequent cause of mischief to us it is because we let it act independently of the will's control--in which case it is sure to become the slave of the senses. Separated from the intelligence, from which it receives light, and from the will, which points out its course of action, the imagination is a blind instinct, precipitous in its movements, impetuous and inconstant in its flights, violent and capricious in its pursuits. It is in constant agitation and torment, passing from one object to another, jumping with a single bound from one extreme to another, from sorrow to joy, from love to hate, from fear to hope.

It magnifies or diminishes things according to the caprice of the moment; and gives a color of sovereign importance to things which in reality are the merest trifles; a word, a look, a sign preoccupies and alarms it; it feasts on suspicion and anxiety, fictitious hopes and deceitful reports; it seizes with avidity on the things that please it, but scarcely is it in possession of the sought for objects when it abandons them with disgust. Hence the impressions to which it gives rise are as whimsical and as inconstant as itself; they appear and disappear in the soul without any apparent reason for their presence or absence.

The woman, whose imagination has been developed at the expense of her other faculties, may be said to lead a dreamy, fictitious, contentious and agitated life. This state is rendered still more dangerous by the agreeable forms which it assumes, and which flatter the mind and senses by their rapid and constant changes. Hence it is that women endowed with this doleful gift have the sad privilege of drawing around them persons of volatile minds and inconstant hearts. They invariably finish by becoming the dupes of their own fickle impressions, and are taken in the snares in which their vanity sought to inveigle others.

Could you but see the living tableau of one of those souls tyrannized by the imagination, the sight would arouse both your compassion and disgust; for hers is a fickle, inconstant, fretful and worried life. During the long dreary days not a single instant is completely and sincerely given to God. Her thoughts, affections, desires and occupations never rise above trivialness. Among the multitude of persons of her acquaintance there is not a single one whom she sincerely loves, or to whom she can render herself amiable. In the multiplied interviews to which she has devoted her life-time not a single genuine affection can be found: words which the lips pronounce and which the heart ignores; visits made through etiquette or inspired by frivolity; conversations that are mutually indulged in for mutual illusion or deception;--such are the joys, such the occupations, of this woman.

With dispositions such as these there cannot be question of sincere piety nor of a Christian spirit. Piety resides in the will and supposes the love of duty; imagination abhors duty and seeks only after pleasure. True, the grace of God is all-powerful, it is not tied down to the development of our natural qualities, and God knows well, when He pleases, how to come to the assistance of the soul's faculties, and plant the germs of solid virtue in a heart that is frivolous and badly disposed; still it is an evident fact that among souls there are some better prepared than others to receive this divine seed, which takes deeper root when the heart is well disposed. Now, among all the agents that can unfit us for the reception of divine grace there is none so bad as an ungoverned imagination, because it is the source, especially among women, of the most fatal illusions.

A woman in this condition spends her whole life-time in deceiving herself and in deceiving others--not purposely, but by a fatal and voluntary illusion; she can see nothing in its true light; all objects appear to her under strange colors; she forms her judgment of them according to the impression they make on the senses, or the effect they produce in the imagination. All this unfits her for the reception of those supernatural truths which fortify the mind without troubling the imagination, and, consequently, she remains insensible to the sweet impressions of grace which acts so mildly on the heart as to be unperceived by the senses. To such a woman piety is a mere matter of form, made up of certain practices which, in the guise of religion, flatter and feed her imagination. But the most terrible feature of this condition is, that it always grows worse, keeping the soul in a cloud of darkness, which even the special light attendant on death cannot dispel.

Thus, living and dying, they deceive themselves, and carry their illusions to the very tribunal of the Sovereign Judge. Then, and not till then, do they discover the truth which, though *seeing*, they did not *perceive* during life. Then, in doleful cries and lamentations will they exclaim, Alas! *"We deceived ourselves, we have gone astray from the path of truth!"*

Do not expose yourself to the same sad fate and doleful end; avoid the danger while it is yet time; train your imagination from a tender age, keep its activity under control,--then, instead of being a source of vile it will be a source of most precious advantages to you.

One of the best means by which you can succeed in doing this is to fortify your will, giving it that authority and consistency which it needs in order to govern the imagination; without a strong will, that remains always self-composed in the midst of the tumult of the senses and the activity of the imagination, you will certainly fail to confine the latter to a just moderation.

That your judgment may enjoy perfect liberty and ease, your every act should be determined during peaceful calmness. Do not forget that, while you are passing through moments of excitement and pre-occupation, you are unable to see things rightly and execute them properly. When in this state of mind a project is proposed to your consideration; you will find that your heart is already fixed upon it before you have duly examined it; then the liberty of your mind becomes shackled either by vain hopes or fears suggested by some blind and violent instinct. In this and similar circumstances you should proceed with great precaution.

It is prudent and wise to defer taking action in any serious matter until self-composure is completely restored, until the mind is serene, the heart at peace, and the will in full possession of its liberty. Listen not to the plausible solicitations--obey not the impulses of your imagination, but wait several days, or weeks, or even months if necessary; for a final determination taken in the midst of confusion and agitation will inevitably entail bitter regrets. Even prayer will not obtain for you, while in such a state of mind, all the light that you need. What you should first ask is, that God would lull this storm, and restore peace to your soul; but it is not the moment to pray that He may inspire you what to do in this or that difficulty, because, preoccupied as you are, you will perhaps take for the voice of God and of your conscience the cries of your troubled imagination.

When, after a mature and serious examination of the matter at issue, you have calmly discovered what course to adopt, it is then time to enlist the service of the imagination to aid your will, and get it interested in the work that you have to do, in order to impart new energy to the soul, and new light to the intelligence; when it is docile to the orders of the will it is a powerful auxiliary for good.

Never forget that the liberty of the mind and heart is an indispensable condition to judge rightly, to love with security, and to act with prudence; and that whatever tends to diminish this liberty should arouse your suspicions, no matter what may be its apparent advantages; for these can never equal the advantages accruing from an unshackled heart and mind.

CHAPTER XI.
PIETY.

Most appropriately indeed was the name *piety* given by our fathers in the faith to the sentiment which elevates the mind and heart to God. It establishes an intimate union between God and the Christian soul, for it is an affection composed of the most generous qualities of the human heart. In woman, it is a mixture of respect, devotedness and tenderness, which are enhanced still more by a certain blending of fear, confidence, and candor. Man is pious towards God and his parents; but the woman whose heart is not vitiated by anything fictitious is pious towards those whom she loves, for in each one of her affections may be found, combined in different degrees, all the shades of sentiment that we have mentioned above; but it is in her piety towards God that they are especially striking.

Woman's heart languishes for God, because it thirsts after the good and beautiful; and all her efforts to satisfy its cravings will prove futile until it is immersed in the bosom of the Divinity, the Source of all goodness and beauty. With woman the heart is the great receptacle of grace, the principal agent in the practice of piety and virtue. If this precious disposition of her heart offers many and great advantages, it carries with it also its inconveniences. The heart is a near neighbor of the imagination, and the latter often allures the former by its charms. Its activity is often developed and exercised at the expense of the will, by diminishing and enfeebling the power and influence of the latter. It not unfrequently happens that the heart becomes the seat of dangerous illusions, when it not only favors, but even indulges in that tender and sensible piety, which is founded on and fed by lively sentiments and beautiful images. In this state it costs no little effort to will and act.

The reading of a pious book, the meditating on the mysteries of the passion and death of our Saviour will melt the heart to tenderness. Thus, nature has a greater share than grace in piety and fervor of this stamp. Self-complacency and self-love are here most adroitly concealed under the garb of humility, and it requires a rare sagacity to discover their presence. The Christian soul in this state seeks not to please God or others, but it seeks rather its own pleasure, and for many women this kind of piety is a form of affectation and vanity. With those fine sentiments and enthusiastic transports they remain unmortified, vain and curious lovers of flattery and averse to reproof, retaining all their faults, which they endeavor to conceal under the mask of external piety.

Do not ask such women to bridle their will or to restrain the sallies of their humor,--speak not to them of the good derived from self-mortification, self-abnegation and the love of the Cross,--words such as these have no signification for them. They are satisfied with simply feeling and giving expression to those virtues, after the manner of artists who, by a happy disposition of mind, are expert in becoming penetrated with ideas and sentiments in which their will has no part whatever; and which have no moral influence over their life.

They are delighted to go with Jesus on Mount Tabor and contemplate Him in the splendor of His glory; but when there is question of participating in His ignominy on Calvary they most shamefully abandon Him. And when He asks them to aid Him to carry His cross they do it, if at all, as reluctantly as did Simon of Cyrene. They willingly multiply prayers and exterior practices of piety, which flatter natural inclinations; they frequent the Sacraments, and this furnishes them the occasion and means of producing those lively and tender sentiments upon which the heart loves to feast.

Their doleful condition is rendered still more deplorable by the use of the most sacred things to nourish their self-love and sensibility. Grace, according to their views of the spiritual life, is only a means to render natural sensibility more delicate and refined. Thus, led on from one delusion to another, such women come to the end of their life, rich in foliage and flowers, but without ever having produced any fruit.

I hope, dear reader, that such may not be your case; but, to avoid all error on a point of such vital interest, meditate constantly on the divine instructions that Jesus has left us in the Sacred Scriptures, and on those also with which He inspired the pious author of the "Following of Christ," their most perfect commentator. Learn to discern genuine piety from that which bears only the name. Learn to distinguish between its object and that which is only a means to attain that object,--two things which are frequently and erroneously confounded, yet which are very distinct and very different from each other; for it is a great mistake to neglect the end by attaching too much importance to the means by which to attain it.

Piety does not consist in sublime language, mystical thoughts, or angelical sentiments, for, according to St. Paul, we might speak the language of angels and be still only sounding brass; neither does it consist in the knowledge of divine mysteries, nor in the more excellent intellectual gifts; for, according to the same apostle, a man might be a prophet and possess a knowledge of all science, without being on that account anything in the sight of God.

Faith is truly grand, because it is the principal basis of our justification; and because with it we are enabled to obtain all things from God. Nevertheless, man might have faith strong enough to move mountains and be absolutely nothing before God. Charity to the poor, compassion for the unfortunate are indeed excellent virtues, because they cancel numerous sins, and because they seem to form the principal matter of that terrible judgment which will decide our weal or woe for eternity; yet you might distribute all your wealth among the poor, and still merit no reward from God.

We are recommended by the Holy Scriptures and by the masters of the spiritual life to practice mortification, the perfection of which is found in martyrdom; and nevertheless, though you should even lacerate your body till it became one bleeding wound, and deliver it into the hands of the executioner to be burned, you might gain nothing thereby.

None of all those things constitutes the essence of piety. One thing alone can claim this privilege and that is CHARITY, not that charity which consists merely in *feeling* and *speaking*, but a *charity that is active*, and which penetrates the entire life by its divine, influence; that charity which is patient and beneficent, not envious, dealing not perversely, not puffed up. True charity is not ambitious seeks not its own, is not provoked to anger, thinks no evil, does not rejoice in iniquity but for the good it beholds everywhere, it bears all things, believes all things, hopes all things and endures all things; such is the soul of true piety according to the Apostle

St. Paul. (Cor. I Epist., xiii chap.)

Our divine Lord clearly defines its nature in the following terms: "***If any man will come after me, let him deny himself, and take up his cross, and follow me, for he that will save his life, shall lose it, and he that shall lose his life for my sake shall find it.***" (Matth. ch. xvi.) To be a Christian consists in walking in the footsteps of Jesus Christ. Hence, to follow Him and carry the cross, self-denial is the first and most necessary qualification. In order to enjoy the eternal happiness of the future life we must sacrifice the false joys of earth. Again, He tells us: "***The kingdom of heaven suffereth violence, and the violent bear it away***," that is to say, ***the valiant, the energetic, and persevering***, will alone succeed in securing it; for the words ***bear away*** express the action of one that seizes a prey. Add to these texts those others of St. Paul: ***"If any man have not the spirit of Christ, he is none of his,"*** that is--he does not belong to Christ, he is not His disciple; and ***"they that are Christ's have crucified their flesh with the vices and concupiscences."***

Now I would not have you think that the piety of which I speak is too elevated for you, that it can he practiced only by members of religious orders, and very holy laics--this is by no means the case. What is required of you is nothing more than what our Lord and all the saints would have you do.

I must point out another error not less pernicious to the practice of true piety, namely; that of taking the means to the acquisition of piety as the end for which you practice it, for the means should at all times be appreciated according to their just value, or according to the assistance they give you to attain your end as a true Christian, which consists in dying to self and to self-glory. I would not have you judge of your progress in perfection by the number of your communions, or the multitude of your pious practices, or the length of your prayers, but by the victories which you gain over yourself, over your passions, your character, and your temper.

Like all other good things, you can turn prayer to your spiritual detriment, when you have recourse to it through vain glory. Be thoroughly convinced of the truth expressed by the Evangelist St. John, ***that he is a liar who says that he loves God, and does not keep his commandments.*** Remember that the spirit of darkness, as St. Paul tells us, can, and often does, transform himself into an angel of light, and produce in the mind false lights, which dazzle and blind it.

Now that you know in what the essence of piety consists, you ought to learn in what faculty of the soul it resides, and this knowledge will preserve you from many illusions, and point out to you the direction in which you must advance in order to attain your end.

Piety, should, by its divine influence, penetrate all the faculties of the soul and take possession of your whole being; it ought, as we have said above, to make its presence especially felt in your heart, by purifying all its affections; but its principal abode should be in the will, through which it may reach all the other faculties in order to elevate and vivify them.

The will is, indeed, if I may so speak, the organ or the instrument of sacrifice and duty; and since piety properly consists in sacrifice and duty, in suppressing the inordinate appetites of the human heart, and elevating nature above herself, the will is the faculty in which piety should reside.

It is not an easy matter to be truly pious, for, in order to attain to a superior order of spiritual perfection, we must lay aside *self* which paralyzes all the generous movements of the soul,-- we must also faithfully correspond to divine grace. All this entails much difficulty, many struggles, and, consequently, great and constant efforts.

Every being has a tendency, founded on an imperious instinct, to dwell in its natural sphere, which it can not leave even to enter a superior one without making a great effort. Hence, the Holy Ghost warns him who desires to serve God to prepare for temptation and struggle. Now, among all the faculties of the soul, the will is the best disposed for the combat, because pleasure has a smaller share in its movements than in those of the heart and imagination; it is able, when necessary, to rise superior to the most alluring charms, preferring fidelity to duty with all its difficulties and bitterness.

To be pious implies the faithful observance of God's commandments, *"If you love me,"* says Christ, *"keep my commandments;"* it consists in being resigned to the will of God, ready to be disposed of at His good pleasure. To do this you must place all your faculties, and especially your will at His disposal. God has reserved to Himself the right of acting in an intimate and profound manner upon the will. This faculty is His sanctuary, in which He delights to dwell, and operate the prodigies of His grace and love, which He communicates with unbounded prodigality to His elect.

This is the throne upon which He silently engraves the image of His divine Son, the essential characteristic of predestination. It is in this power of the human soul that He plants in the depth of Christian humility the foundation of solid virtue, in defiance to the disorders of the mind, the agitations of the heart and the incoherencies of the memory.

From the bosom of the Divinity our Blessed Lord brought with Him two special favors, one of which was for His eternal Father, and the other to be given persons of good-will. He charged His angels to announce them to the world in the person of the shepherds. They were, glory for His Father and peace for men, but only for men of good- will. This heavenly peace is a foretaste of the never-ending joys of Paradise. It is a prize worth striving for, and easy to secure, at least for you, since it is promised to all persons of good-will.

CHAPTER XII.
VOCATION.

God, who has created all things by His own power, conserves them by an act of His divine love; and by His providence leads them to their appointed destiny through ways conformable to their own nature. He did not create man to live a solitary being, and, consequently, implanted in his heart an instinctive need of society; desiring that the latter should effectively contribute to the development of the faculties of soul and body. And, as society cannot subsist without a certain variety of conditions, and functions, which lend each other mutual aid, He has planted in our souls certain dispositions in harmony with the particular state of life to which He has destined us. This is what is called *vocation*.

It is, as you perceive, only a particular form of that general providence by which God governs the universe, giving to the lilies their eclat and perfume, watching with maternal care over the young brood, preparing its food for the little bird, and not allowing a single hair to fall from our heads without His permission. I purposely make use of the beautiful images that Jesus Himself employed to reveal to us the sweet mystery of providence.

To deny that man has a special vocation is placing him in a rank inferior to the plants and irrational animals. It is denying the variety of dispositions which enter into the combination of character, and which is at once one of the greatest charms of and most precious advantages to society; it is forcing on the mind the conviction that every one is free to choose, whether in or out of season, his post in the world, even when such a course would be contrary to the principles of common-sense, and would entail the subversion of society; for, let each and every one be directed in the choice of his post by the whims and caprices of nature, assuredly society will soon become demoralized, even as an army in which each soldier would be free to choose and take the grade and position that best suited his tastes.

If society is kept in a constant feverish agitation, by the furious contests of ungoverned passion, it is because no one, or at least the vast number never take the trouble to consult God by prayer, or otherwise, before making a choice of a state of life. If there are so many dissatisfied with their state of life it is because they are not where God had destined them to be. If life is blighted with deception, fraught with regrets and bitterness, if our fairest hopes are blasted, if pain and sorrow brood over our existence, it is because the soul suffers the punishment entailed by her levity or negligence in a matter on which her weal or woe depends, both for time and eternity.

Oh, how sadly rare in the world is that sweet and celestial peace, that interior contentment, that pure and simple joy which in holier times families prized as their most precious inheritance; and which they handed down to their posterity as one of their richest gifts: then the thought of God and eternity presided over all the important actions of their life; then the light of heaven was invoked when there was question of any important undertaking; and as grave matters were considered and weighed in the light of truth and religion, due attention was paid to the choice of a state of life.

They knew that, while other proceedings might be changed, and consequently their fatal result averted when foreseen, the step made in the choice of a state of life is irrevocable and a mistake made in that step not only involves our happiness or misery for time but also for eternity. Hence it is said by many that vocation is closely allied with predestination.

It is a most solemn moment in the Christian's life, for it is the beginning of that road by which he must attain his destination. At this juncture it is consoling to consider with the eye of faith, the love and solicitude with which God protects the soul; to behold Jesus offering with ineffable tenderness for her the blood which He shed on the cross. To see the guardian angel redoubling his charitable efforts in the interest of his client, awaiting with pious anxiety the issue of a deliberation upon which must depend in a great measure the success or failure of his labors for her eternal salvation.

Still, should any one be so unfortunate as to make a bad choice, let him not consider his condition irremediable; divine mercy has inexhaustible resources from which to provide us with the means to work out our salvation, and prevent the doleful consequences of those fatal errors.

Yet, it is certain beyond all question, that we render the work of our eternal salvation always more difficult when we have not embraced that state of life which God had laid out for us; for the sins which are a consequence of this want of correspondence to the divine will, will have, if not a decisive influence, at least a considerable share in the work of our reprobation. How many souls now writhing in eternal torments could, on ascending the course of their lives, point out the solemn moment in which they made a choice of a state of life as the time of their departure from the road to heaven.

No Christian who has his salvation at heart will hesitate to say that it is folly to treat with indifference and levity a matter of such vital importance; for he must remember with a sacred awe that, when he makes a choice of a state of life, he pronounces in a certain manner an irrevocable sentence on himself.

When the soul is deprived of the advantages of a rule of life, of the advantages of good dispositions, character and temperament, as well as of those provided by circumstances, men and things on the one hand; and when she is obliged to struggle incessantly against herself and external obstacles on the other hand, the work of her salvation becomes more difficult and less certain. In this deplorable condition, the only pillar left her on which she can anchor her hopes of salvation is the mercy of God; but then a faithful correspondence with divine grace in the most minute details, constant and persevering prayer to obtain strength to bear the trials of life with profit, are positively necessary conditions to escape destruction.

Commencing her career, woman finds for the most part only two roads that dispute the choice of her adoption. Estranged, generally speaking, to the professional life, or at least, acting in it only a secondary role, she scarcely gives it a serious thought; she can therefore give all due deliberation to her choice between marriage and celibacy.

If all were bound to choose the more perfect state, considered in itself, the question would be easily settled, as in that case there would be, properly speaking, no choice to make; for evidently it is the celibate state of life that should be adopted, since it is a more perfect state than that of marriage; and the church, maintaining the doctrine of the Apostle on this point, has condemned as heretics those who teach that the married state is as perfect as that of virginity. But, if all should aspire to perfection, if all are free to choose the kind of life that will better insure the attaining of that perfection, then all are not obliged to embrace the celibate state, since our perfection consists in doing God's will.

When you are about to make a choice of a state of life, you are not only permitted, but even urged, to take into consideration your dispositions and aptitudes for the state which you propose to embrace; and, if they are in good accord with it, you may safely conjecture that they were given you for that state of life. Your imperative duty consists in distinguishing between the call given by God and the voice of passion or prejudice. Hence you should promptly and faithfully follow the attractions and dispositions that God has given you, and nothing else.

If for instance, a woman made her choice with a view of pandering to her vanity, curiosity, worldly love, or some other passion still more culpable perhaps, God would have no part in her determinations, and she would inevitably become the dupe of her own folly; for God gives light only to such as are sincere in their search for it, and they who look for it in this way are such as those, who, in examining the question of their vocation, have chiefly in view the glory of God and their own salvation.

If the natural dispositions should be taken into consideration, it is not indeed with a view to flatter nature and avoid the struggles incident to the Christian life. That would be renouncing the glorious title of Christian, and the incomparable favor that God has conferred upon us in creating us to live with Him forever. If it is useful to consult our taste and aptitude it is because they are for the most part indicative of God's will; hence we ought to employ them for the purpose for which He gave them to us. Then the object of your researches in this matter should be to discover God's will in that state of life for which He has given you a pronounced taste and aptitude; but, because the caprice of nature or character may sometimes be taken for that taste and aptitude, you are not altogether safe from deception without some other guarantee.

It frequently happens that man believes to be an inspiration from God what is only the effect of badly-regulated passion or some bad habit deeply rooted in the soul. In order to be sure that God has given such a disposition or aptitude of the heart and mind as being indicative of the state of life He would have us enter, it should be possessed of the following conditions, namely: The sanction of time, which is the instrument that God ordinarily employs to stamp the impress of His will on the works that He operates in us. It is necessary that this disposition has been constant, that is to say, that it has not suffered from frequent or long interruptions. A transitory taste appearing to-day and vanishing to-morrow, a volatile inclination frequently appearing and just as frequently disappearing, merits no consideration in an affair that involves the Christian's happiness both for time and eternity.

However, if the aptitude which you feel in your soul for a given state of life has lost much of its vivacity, or even when it should have frequently vanished in the course of your life; you are in duty bound to study the causes and circumstances of this change, especially when, with the disappearence of that inclination, piety and fervor in God's service have also diminished in the soul.

If, as often as you felt the sweet impulse of divine grace in prayer and holy communion this inclination became also aroused in the soul; if you felt it increase in proportion as you gave yourself to God, you may safely conclude that it is the indicator of God's will in your regard, and that its vascillating or enfeebled condition was the work of your own perverse will. Hence, in order to ascertain whether the natural inclination or aptitude you feel for any state of life is from God or the effect of a deluded fancy, you need but compare your natural aptitude with those you have received through divine grace; and if you find them in perfect accord you may rest assured that they are from God, for He is the author of nature as well as of grace. On the contrary, should they disagree then you may safely conclude that your natural desire or inclination is a delusion.

This last consideration should not be omitted, especially when there is question of embracing the religious life; for the attraction by which we feel ourselves drawn to a more perfect life is in itself a gift of God, and one of His most precious gifts. As often as this attraction reveals its presence in the heart, it singularly involves the study of vocation. Hence, it is a most delicate and perilous matter to deal with, for if this attraction comes from God and if the soul repels it she prepares for herself lamentable delusions, and a life fraught with bitterness and remorse. God has a reason for frequently saying in the Sacred Scriptures that He is a jealous God, and the church, for the same reason, addresses Jesus in the litanies, *jealous of souls*.

Hence, after having shown the greatest preference for a soul, in honoring her with the exalted dignity of being His spouse, adorning her with the gorgeous splendor of His richest treasures, and then see Himself basely rejected, or treated with cold indifference; His divine justice should naturally revenge the insult; which is done by delivering her into her own hands, the most cruel punishment that could be inflicted on her.

However, if you feel an attraction for the religious life, it, would be imprudent and rash on your part to decide the matter yourself. You should, in the spirit of humility, after having consulted God by prayer, consult some enlightened persons noted for their wisdom and prudence, piety and learning, who will advise you with a view to secure the spiritual welfare of your soul above all things. Should those to whom you address yourself fail to give all the assurance you should have, be not backward in consulting others; for unlimited confidence in the words of any man, no matter who he may be, will not dispense you from all responsibility before God, nor preserve you from making a wrong choice.

Neither should you lose sight of, or derogate in the least, from the respect and obedience you owe your parents. It is their sacred duty and right to advise you; and to whom should you look for a more disinterested advice? A young girl would indeed be an object of pity if, instead of finding a truly Christian tenderness in her parents, they would be her idolizers so far as to be blinded to her true interests. It is for this blind and foolish love that many parents sacrifice their children, either by ignoring their just claims to embrace the religious life, or by opposing an advantageous marriage through vanity or personal interest.

CHAPTER XIII.
A SERIOUS MIND.

A vast number of people unfortunately labor under the false impression that woman's great work and duty consists in making her company agreeable and pleasing to all. This error is most prejudicial to woman; it is opposed to the teachings of religion and the Holy Scriptures; and nevertheless it is only too true that a countless number of women have sedulously labored for its propagation, or, at least, they have proved by their actions that this is their *only* work; and in many places, to the great detriment of society, the education of girls has been directed in a great measure according to this false opinion.

They are taught to esteem graceful manners, elegance of deportment, flashy humor, affability of character, and unlimited condescension as being the elements of a finished education; and the precious days of childhood with the more precious time of adolescence have been entirely absorbed to acquire it.

This is the school that has given birth to what is called "*Arts of Pleasure*," to which it sacrifices the knowledge of more necessary things which instruct the mind, fortify the heart, and invigorate the will. Our compassion and disgust are simultaneously aroused, when we see so many women whose education has given them no other knowledge than to teach them how to flatter the taste of others at the expense of Christian modesty.

How many women there are who, from their youth, have renounced the dignity and glorious privileges of their sex, calmly resigning themselves to play the inferior and humiliating role that the prejudices and passions of a frivolous society impose upon them!

It is our heart-felt desire that you may never experience anything of the kind; suffer not the aureola with which God has decorated your brow to be ruthlessly removed and trampled under foot. Remember that your soul is just as noble as that of man; that it is illuminated by the same faith, drawn towards heaven by the same hopes, and united to the same Author of all greatness and of all life by the same charity. Should your belief in this waver, transport yourself in spirit to Calvary: there you will see that women were the only sympathizers of Jesus, and, while hanging on the cross, women were, with the exception of St. John, the only witnesses of His death.

The apostles and disciples, all had fled; and in this memorable scene in which all things seem to be confounded courage and valor seemed to have taken refuge in the soul of women. Hence the Church records, with love and gratitude, on the brightest pages of her history, this noble and generous act of devotedness as being the special privilege of your sex, since it was won on the ever-memorable day of our redemption.

It is not easy to look a painful truth in the face; but we are forced to do so when we reluctantly confess that female frivolity is the source of that levity which prevails now-a-days, to such an extent as to affect the very laws and government of society. To keep aloof from this poisonous atmosphere, you must cultivate that serious turn of mind, that gravity which gives women an air of majesty, and wins the homage of those who do not even understand her.

Experience will teach you that the importance attached to the seriousness with which woman's life should be enveloped is undervalued. Learn to appreciate it as it merits; show that appreciation by now giving to all the actions of your life that weight and gravity which shall render them agreeable to God.

To succeed in your good resolution great firmness is required; you will be obliged to condemn the frivolity of young persons in whose company circumstances may throw you. You must set your face against the fashions of the world, against the force of habit and prejudice, perhaps against the freaks of your own character. But remember that the reward awaiting you is well worth the struggle you are asked to sustain; and this struggle will not be so difficult as you may think, if you face it courageously, coherently and perseveringly, employing, of course, the proper means.

To begin, you should cast overboard that inclination to frivolity wherever you meet with it. But since a bad plant is more quickly and radically destroyed by pulling it out of the roots than by simply lopping of the tops as they appear over ground, so do we likewise succeed better in correcting a bad habit, or destroying an evil inclination by attacking it at its source than by being satisfied with arresting its bad effects, allowing the cause to remain. And since it is in the mind that frivolity takes up its abode, it is there that it must be sought for and destroyed.

There exists among the different faculties of the soul a certain order, a species of hierarchy which gives a certain preponderance to some of them over the others; consequently some of them are of an inferior while others are of a superior order. You will labor in vain to give a serious cast to your sentiments and actions if you feed your mind on frivolous thoughts, while serious thoughts are the progenitors of enduring affections and noble deeds. Hence the culture of the mind is an important factor to the acquisition of a taste for those things which are the true ornament of woman. Sentiments are the outcomings of thoughts, and both together are expressed by actions.

Feed your intelligence with serious thoughts; never amuse it with those trifles which absorb the attention of persons of your age. Do not think that those serious thoughts badly become your youth; that they would deprive you of a part of your comfort, rendering you wearisome to others and insupportable to yourself; that they would give you a pedantic and affected air which would lead others to believe that you despised them; that every age has its peculiar tastes and customs, and that it would be an act of uncalled-for severity to exact from a young person just beginning, so to say, the apprenticeship of life, a gravity of manners and dispositions that would scarcely be required at a maturer age.

Seriousness is required in all ages, but not always in the same degree. Thus the gravity befitting a young lady is very different from that expected from a woman more advanced in years. This virtue, far from excluding legitimate amusement and pleasure, only regulates and elevates them by confining them to just limits. An agreeable and lively turn may be given to the most serious things, rendering them pleasing and acceptable to the minds of all.

Truth is never subtle, and never darkens the soul in which it resides; on the contrary, it sheds a halo of light around her, revealing all those interior movements which lend a sweet and amiable charm to every action.

You would be the first to condemn the doctrine of those who maintain that woman must be of a frivolous turn of mind in order to be agreeable. You would justly regard, as an outrage to your sex, such assertions as go to show that serious-ness can have no place in the mind of woman. Such being the case, you will not say, with many of your age, that the time will come soon enough to feed your soul with solid substantial food; and that the age of serious thoughts will come only too soon; nor will you close your eyes to the fact, taught by long experience, that every one must reap in riper years such fruit as they had sown in youth. If you wait till then, it will be too late for you to enter another groove and form new habits. If you are now frivolous in your thoughts and sentiments you will be so later; for, as age fortifies the tastes and inclinations, frivolity must increase as you advance in years.

Perhaps facts of this nature have already fallen under your notice; you must have met with old ladies whose levity so painfully contrasts with the gravity that becomes their age; and, while it is not permitted us to judge others, yet every good Christian must be shocked at this contrast. Profit by their example, sad as it is, and hasten to conclude that it is folly to defer to a future time what can and should be done at present; and that defects, as well as virtue, are fortified by time and habit. If your early education has not been truly Christian, if the teachings of divine faith have not yet rendered you familiar with the most serious things of life, you might perhaps consider as difficult, or even impracticable, the counsels that I give you now.

Is there anything more serious or more in opposition to our natural inclina-tions, and at the same time less consistent with the deplorable levity of our minds, than the truths of our holy religion? For serious, indeed, must be the reflections that those truths inspire, which you should now learn to meditate seriously, in order to make them a life-long practice. Is it not a serious occupation of the mind to think of God, of the salvation of your soul, the briefness of life, eternity which follows it, the duties that religion imposes upon you? Is it not a serious occupation to address God in holy prayer, to descend into the secret folds of your conscience, and examine all your actions in the light of the gospel; to reveal in all your works the sacred charac-ter that you have received in baptism; to lead a life according to the spirit of faith, and not according to the spirit of the world-for, if there is no difference between your conduct and that of worldlings, to what purpose will the title of Christian avail you? All this is a serious work, and requires a serious mind to accomplish it.

The practice of Christian virtues supposes and develops at the same time the love of seriousness. This love does not increase in a superficial soul; while it is entirely sterile in a frivolous mind. Remember that you have now attained the age between childhood and womanhood, when it is no longer lawful to be amused by trifles, and when you are called upon to prepare for austere duties which you must, ere long, discharge.

You have now come to that period of life at which you must determine your final future course; hence you have need of a serious mind and will to guide you securely in the choice of the road, as also to pave it with those virtues which in the end will form your most precious treasures. This road will be such as you have made it, narrow or wide, level or rough, according to the pains and labor that you have expended in preparing it.

If you hearken to the voice of reason, and wish to profit by the lessons of wisdom, you will not squander a most precious time in vain amusements; you will neither step to the right nor to the left, but continue right on in the way of stern duty. The world's siren charms will have no attraction for you, as their bitter fruits would extort from you bitter regrets for having so little profited by the most precious time of your life.

Oh, how sorrowful the old age of women who have never nourished their minds otherwise than with frivolous thoughts: finding neither in themselves nor in society any means to dispel the gloom that envelops them, and not being able to enlist the sympathy of the world which abandons and despises them, they are condemned to eke out a miserable existence in the disgust and wearisomeness of a sombre solitude.

To a serious woman, on the contrary, old age lends a peculiar charm which renders her company agreeable to, and sought for, by all serious minds. Her conversation and manners still possess all the blitheness, freshness and vivacity of youth. Her steady lightsome gaze, tempered by a benignant and reflective mind, lends her an air of amiability and majesty. Her language is instructive, her counsels encouraging, while her reproaches arouse the heart to a sense of duty. She has friends wherever she is known, friends who revere and respect, without idolizing her. In her youth she never pandered to flattery, now, old, she shall not experience ingratitude. The friends she earned by her sterling worth will recall to her mind the happy souvenirs of her youth, even up to the last days of her life; for her years bear with them all their primitive charms which can never decline under the influence of time, because the thoughts and affections that produced and preserved them are now what they were, solid and grave. And while the companions of her youth languish and fret in their sad isolation, she, always the same, sees herself surrounded by a multitude, anxious to profit by her experience.

If you have learned to be serious in youth, you shall enjoy an agreeable old age; but if the former be stamped with levity and frivolity, the latter shall be fraught with sorrow and desolation. Do not count on the charms of youth, it is a flower that shall very soon fade, and like a bird on the wing, shall leave no trace behind it. The lustre of your eyes now beaming delight shall soon grow dull; the bloom shall depart from your cheek; the bright hopes that now fill your soul shall give place to sad souvenirs; and your heart which is now the abode of delight shall then be harrowed with sorrow and woe. To-day you are flattered and praised, then you shall be a castaway, abandoned. All that will remain to you is God and your soul, with whom you had never learned to converse or commune. Oh, sad, indeed, is the old age of a frivolous youth!

CHAPTER XIV.
CHOICE OP COMPANIONS.

Since a predisposition to good and evil is found among persons of all classes and ages; and as this predisposition is especially strong at your age, when the sympathies are most tender, when the heart so candid and open is ready to receive and reciprocate those secret emanations that escape from the souls of loved ones; you require to take more than ordinary precautions, since the danger to which these circumstances expose you is indeed very great, and requires a prudence superior to your years,--you must therefore look for it in the advice of others, but more especially in that of your mother who should be your first adviser in all things.

How many women owe to the examples and deceptive lessons of a so- called friend, the bitterness that corrodes their hearts, and the remorse which perhaps torments their life! We pass over in silence those societies the evident danger of which is easily perceived, and on that account easily averted; but you have not the same guarantee against the noxious effects which arise from those relations whose union is found in the most frivolous instincts of the heart, to which access is gained by the feeblest faculties of the soul. What is it that is most commonly found in those intimacies, if not thoughts without consistency, vain hopes, precocious or impatient desires, indiscreet confidence, imprudent language, rash questions and answers rasher still?

As a general rule, any society or company from which you derive no benefit for head or heart is, if not dangerous, at least pernicious; and you ought to shun them unless that imperative reasons or the will of your parents advise otherwise; for all that tends to diminish your esteem for the value of time and for the love of serious things is prejudicial to your soul. You should prefer your mother's company to that of all others. Her life should be as a book constantly open before you; her lessons and examples, her experience and counsels should be an inexhaustible mine of instruction, useful and precious to your soul.

The young lady is indeed an object of compassion who feels her mother's company irksome and onerous. At your age the heart is confiding and effusive, and it needs some bosom in which to repose its confidence; for it would be subjecting it to an ordeal too rude, and exposing it perhaps to a fatal reaction, by completely depriving it of consolations derived from acquaintances approved by every law, human and divine. It should be treated with moderation, founded on prudence, as undue severity renders its desires and needs more imperative.

But if it is dangerous to restrict the heart to silence and inaction it is much more dangerous to feed it on frivolous affections. There is nothing that exhausts its energies so much as an over-indulgence in those puerile sentiments fed by the imagination. Those sentiments create within it a void which nothing can fill, and destroy its love for everything that is noble and generous.

A frivolous heart is not less disastrous to woman than is a frivolous mind. How many women find themselves disarmed and powerless in important circumstances of life, for having neglected in youth the training of the heart's affections! How many are unequal to the task of discharging a painful duty, because they were wont to seek their pleasure in all they did from early childhood! How many who, spite of the chastisement of adversity and deception incurred by their idolizing preference for their levity and affections, still remain the dupes of their blind attachment even in their old age! Your esteem for your own heart, and appreciation for its affections, should be highly noteworthy, and deeply graven in your mind by the constant habit of prizing them.

When you feel an attraction for a young person of your own age, do not blindly obey it, before having maturely studied its nature and motives. We should always act for a purpose worthy of ourselves, but more especially so when there is question of delivering ourselves over to the confidence and friendship of others; for in this mutual exchange we dispose of the greater part of our being. In this intimate relation, which is formed insensibly by repeated interviews, there is formed a reciprocal discernment that exercises a powerful influence over all the faculties of the soul, the convictions of the minds, the sentiments of the heart, the habits of character, and often even over the general deportment.

The good sense of our fathers has expressed this truth by one of those proverbs so familiar to them: "*Tell me your company and I know who you are.*" Of course you have frequently heard those words, and knowing their meaning withal, perhaps you have not considered the circumstances wherein they may be applied. We earnestly wish that they may never be employed relative to you, at the expense of the joy of your heart or the peace of your conscience.

You should use much discretion in the choice that you make of the person with whom you would form an intimate acquaintance; for such an intimacy is not only founded on a mutual confidence, and reciprocal affections; it is also the result which follows from being frequently in each other's company. This latter intimacy is more dangerous than the former because the heart, not thinking itself interested, is less upon its guard, and consequently more exposed to suffer from the poison concealed in words and examples.

Be assured of the nature of the attraction you feel. See if it is founded upon solid qualities, capable of making an impression upon an upright and serious mind, or upon those superficial qualities which the world esteems, and which allure volatile minds. In the latter case, you cannot, without danger, engage in relations; the inevitable effect of which must be either to fortify your present defects, or add to them others which you have not at present. If your love for any one be founded on trivial motives, and if you dispense yourself from the obligation of restraining your affections, let me entreat you to take at least all the precautions that prudence requires to prevent you from becoming the dupe of a foolish fondness. But if your affections are founded on sympathy of character, on a concurrence of holy thoughts and sentiments, with a view to strengthen the love and practice of virtue; then the attainment of their object is highly commendable and praiseworthy; and you may justly hope to secure the happiest results from it. But even then, you should be on your guard against your own judgment, placing a certain restraint on your sentiments of confidence and love, or friendship, which, in order to be lasting, must be calm, devoid of that impetuosity which acts violently on the heart. It should be the work of time, shedding its sweet influence on the duties of life, rendering their accomplishment less laborious and more fruitful.

Those who love each other with a sincere Christian affection, willingly sacrifice to duty the pleasure of being together, or rather their great pleasure consists in doing God's will; with noble courage they rise superior to all other considerations, and mutually inspire each other with a holy zeal, imposing silence upon the voice of their affections, in presence of the voice of their conscience.

Such is the manner in which persons should love each other; such are the affections that God blesses and rewards. You are deeply indebted to Divine Providence if it has sent you one whom you can love in this way, for this is one of the most precious gifts of God's mercy. It is especially at your age that such friendships are most easily formed, because then the heart is more tender and confiding. How many women owe, in a great measure, their peace of mind and conscience to the good advice and protecting influence of a friend whom they met with in the springtime of life.

There are in woman's life many delicate and trying circumstances that demand the intervention of a sincere friend, to direct and sustain her, when the light of conscience becomes obscured or extinct; when the energies of the heart succumb to the allurements of pleasure; when the mind, embarrassed by doubt and perplexity, can scarcely distinguish the line of duty, semi-obliterated by prejudice and passion; happy, then, is the woman who can call upon a faithful and tried friend, to whom she can confide the secrets of her heart, and from whom she may hope to receive the help and consolation that her condition calls for.

CHAPTER XV.
TOILET.

An undue attention to toilet is a dangerous rock for many women who, otherwise remarkable for their grave deportment, are sometimes greater slaves than the most frivolous women to dress and fashion. It is truly a great misery to be taken up with undue solicitude for the fragile and perishable part of our being; but more especially so, when such preference is given it by minds which are otherwise noble and elevated. It is painful to be obliged to confess that many women of high and cultivated attainments spend a considerable portion of their life in this futile occupation. It seems incredible that a ribbon-knot, the color of a robe, or the form of a head-dress, could become a capital matter for an intelligent creature destined to contemplate with the angels of heaven the majesty of God.

If there are so few women who enjoy all the advantages of their happy dispositions and attainments, it is because of their inordinate love for toilet and fashion; for nothing narrows the mind or contracts the heart so much as excessive care of the body. When they neglect the soul, the noblest part of man, she revenges herself of the insult by concealing all her brilliant qualities, which alone constitute woman's true beauty and adornment.

It is impossible for a vain or gaudy woman to converse on any serious matter, but she will talk for whole hours on the form or quality of a dress; should the conversation happen to turn on a serious subject, capable of engaging the attention of an elevated mind, her countenance will soon betray a sense of dissatisfaction and weariness.

Give befitting attention to the care of your body, because it is the temple of God, who has deposited therein a precious germ of immortality. But at the same time, keep it in its own place; and since it is the inferior part of your being do not allow it to infringe upon the rights and privileges of the soul, whose docile and obedient servant it should be. Avoid in your toilet all that savors of frivolity, which betray a desire to attract attention; but above all; avoid every thing that might in the least wound modesty. Do not forget that this virtue is one of the most beautiful ornaments of your sex, and that when woman is deprived of it she is like a faded flower, without eclat or perfume. You should conform to the customs of your country and condition without being in any way their slave, remembering that your soul is at all times in duty bound to soar above all those futilities, and conserve by a noble independence, her glory and her majesty.

Do not follow the example of those women who, slaves of the world, obey with blind docility all its caprices; seeking with avidity whatever is novel, in order to be the first in the *fashion*, and acquire by that, the vain reputation of a woman of good taste. Those who believe themselves obliged to have recourse to the seductions of fashion and dress in order to attract the attention of their would-be admirers, give a sad manifestation of the emptiness of their minds and the depravity of their hearts. Those who are distinguished for their noble qualities of head and heart attach their hopes, to loftier claims; by their modesty and reserve they are pleasing to all, and the sentiments which they inspire, being always noble and pure, never give the slightest annoyance to any one; on the contrary they arouse the holiest and most generous instincts of the soul.

One of the sweetest charms that adorns your age is that which arises from its simplicity and candor. The world itself, so liberal in its judgments, will not pardon in you whatever savors of egotism and ostentation. In these and similar things it will avail you naught to offer for excuse custom and usage, behind which so many aged women try to take refuge. Profit, then, by the truce which the world in a measure concedes in favor of your modesty, to acquire the habit of simplicity in your dress and whole exterior. This simplicity, once acquired, will be your guarantee, later on, against the examples and seductions of the fashionable world, which shows as little deference for the laws of good taste as for those of Christian modesty.

The beautiful and good are never in contradiction with each other. The same is true of what are perverse and depraved. And this is why the depravity of taste is in keeping with the standard of a people's moral life. Be assured that there is nothing beautiful except what is true and good; and that there is neither truth nor goodness in things devoid of simplicity. If you regulate your dress and whole exterior bearing according to these two principles you will stand irreproachable to your own conscience, and secure the respect and admiration of the most exacting worldlings, for simplicity of dress and manners possesses charms that win universal approbation.

Never lose sight of your glorious title of Christian. Remember that on the day of your baptism you renounced the pomps and vanities of the world, and, if you are allowed to conform to customs not contrary to the maxims of the Gospel, you ought at the same time manifest in your dress, as in the rest, the glorious character that God has stamped in your soul. You should show by your conduct the striking contrast that exists between the Christian woman and the woman who, being incredulous or indifferent, does not draw her rule of life from the precepts of the Gospel.

Your dress should be grave and modest: these are the characteristic marks by which it can be distinguished from that of women who are slaves of the world. St. Paul said to the Christians of his time: *Let your modesty appear to all men, for the Lord is near you!* What a profound lesson there is in these words, and how strongly they set forth the motives for which a Christian should be modest. To put in practice this counsel of the Apostle, you must accustom yourself to walk in the presence of God, representing to yourself by a lively faith that God is near you, that He sees you and will demand a strict account one day from you of all your actions. Frequently call to mind what St. Paul said to the Corinthians, namely: that *we are a spectacle to men and angels*. Let the true sense of those words sink deeply into your heart, and it will enable you to regulate soul and body.

The desire to attract attention, to draw the admiring gaze of fellow- beings is a weakness that lurks in every human heart; but with woman it seems to be the main-spring to all her actions, which is kept in motion alike by the applause and reproaches of spectators. In the light of faith all this is folly and vanity; for in that light we behold the whole court of heaven, God and His angels watching with an interest full of tenderness and solicitude not only our exterior actions, but even the secret movements of our souls. Could we have a better or more appreciative audience to witness what we do? The very thought of their presence should inspire us with a disgust for those vain desires that urge us to see and be seen by mankind in order to secure to our actions the approbation of the multitude. Regulate your conduct in this matter according to St. Paul's instruction to Timothy: *Let women be clothed in decent apparel, adorning themselves with modesty and sobriety, not with platted hair, or gold or pearls, or costly attire. But, as it becometh women professing godliness, with good works.*

Moreover, you labor under a great mistake if you think that gaudiness in dress is necessary to render you attractive and inspire those sentiments of esteem and affection which sometimes prepare the way to an advantageous alliance. Should you succeed by this means in securing such a marriage, be assured that you deceive yourself; for the man who, setting aside the qualities essential to woman, lets his affections be won by her outward charms only does her an injury, and prepares for her, as well as for himself, bitter regrets in the future. If you fully understand your true interest, both in this life and in the next, far from making your dress a means of attraction, you would tremble to owe to such vile contrivances the affection bestowed on you. You would not compel by your vanity those who love you for your own good to pander to your self-love and encourage your negligence.

The sentiments that a woman awakens in the hearts of her admirers draw their worth from the motives that inspire them, and this being the case, what value shall you set upon affections determined by empty show, and flattered by qualities purely exterior, unworthy of the attention of an intelligent being? Still, for some unaccountable or visionary reason, the greater part of women attach excessive importance to such puerile advantages, and neglect those that are capable of making a deep and lasting impression upon valiant and noble souls. If they are much depreciated in the esteem of those by whom they would like to be loved and admired, the cause may be traced to their own frivolity; let them labor with the same zeal to cultivate the heart and mind that they display upon external show, and they will more readily attract the attention of all who belong to refined and educated society.

CHAPTER XVI.
DESIRE TO PLEASE.

AFTER having created man God saw that it was not good for him to be alone; and in order to console and cheer him in his solitude He took from his side, near his heart, the material out of which He made him a companion. This origin of woman tells us more of her nature, and points out more clearly the end that God proposed to Himself in creating her than the most elaborate and profound treatises or the most lucid theological theories.

Man was made out of the slime of the earth, woman has been formed out of a body already organized and vivified by the breath of life; man has been created to reign over the world, to govern the animals which God placed under his control, woman has been created to be man's companion; to cheer him in his solitude, and share with him the power and gifts which he received from God.

Hence it is quite natural that woman should feel in the depths of her heart a gnawing desire to please and be agreeable, for in that she only obeys the instinct of her nature. Still, woman would be abusing that instinct, and acting contrary to the designs of Providence, if she sought to please by means unworthy of her.

Before plunging Adam into that mysterious sleep, God brought all the animals before him, that he might see and know the extent of his dominion. The sacred writer remarks, that among all those animals Adam did not find a single being that resembled himself. He could find in none of those animals a sociable companion, because none of them had a soul like his, and consequently, could not share in the sweet joy that arises from an interchange of thoughts and sentiments, which constitutes the charming pith of life.

Many of them surpassed him in bodily strength, fleetness and agility, many attracted his attention by the beauty of their form, by their wonderful instinct and industry. And God, through His unbounded goodness, had planted in their very nature a desire or want of attachment, an instinctive gratitude and fidelity, such, that it seemed impossible to desire anything more exquisite of the kind. Still, with all these advantages, man was unsatisfied, he required a being like himself, possessing qualities superior to those found in irrational beings, one with whom his intelligence and heart might commune.

You must have already penetrated the profound sense of the words of the sacred historian and obtained a clear knowledge of the end that God proposed to himself in creating woman. Yes, He has certainly willed that you should be a messenger of consolation and comfort, that your mission should be, not to please and flatter the senses, which the animals did for Adam before Eve was created, but to meet the wants of the mind and heart of man.

Irrational beings suffice to please the senses and imagination; hence, if this is all that you propose to do, you put yourself in contradiction with the designs of God over you, and the grandeur of your destiny. You seem to say to God that it was not necessary for Him to create woman, that man could dispense with her, because the animals subject to his empire sufficed to meet all the wants of his mind and heart. Do not debase and despise your noble nature by thus placing yourself in the same category with animals, which can have nothing in common with the duties of your sublime mission.

The senses are blind, impetuous and changeable in their instincts; inconstancy and change are so necessary to them, that, rather than be condemned to remain immutable, they readily quit a more agreeable object for another very inferior, simply to satisfy that need of change inherent to their nature. Hence the strongest protestations, the most assiduous attentions, and the most active devotedness, though truly sincere in themselves, but when founded on the senses, are like smoke that disappears, even as the material that produces it. You will not have the right even to blame those who may deceive you in this way, because it is not in the power of man to conserve for any notable length of time a sentiment produced by the senses, and which has received no higher sanction than that of the imagination.

The difference, however, between this abortive sentiment and a genuine one is so palpable and characteristic that it is impossible to be mistaken in them, unless that we wilfully close our eyes to the truth. But, alas! it must indeed be confessed that a vast number of women wish to be deceived, not only in their discernment of the sentiment by which they are actuated, but also in their preference for it. And through some unaccountable blindness, they fear every thing that might interfere with their cherished idol. They purposely shut their eyes to the light of truth, preferring to deceive and be deceived than to be obliged, on seeing the matter in its true light, to doubt the power of their frivolous charms; as a proof of this the least compliment paid them for their beautiful or handsome appearance puts them beside themselves so far as to make them forget to consider whether such compliments are authorized by sincerity or flattery.

In vain will you try to convince them that this is not the way in which a genuine sentiment is formed and manifested. It is useless to tell them that such a sentiment does not spring up suddenly in the heart; that, on the contrary, its development is due to the process of a constant and almost insensible growth; being characteristically modest, calm, reserved, and even timid; having God for its first confidential friend, and pure souls for its tutors. It is labor in vain to point out to them that an affection, unaccompanied by the necessary precautions, should be repelled by a young lady as an insult to the dignity of her sex. But they will readily listen to any language that flatters their vanity, which paves the way to so many fatal friendships that often entail a lifetime of woe and sorrow.

When necessity or propriety requires your presence in society, somewhat brilliant, where you must inevitably come in contact with young men whom perhaps you do not know; then you should guard the senses, the mind and the heart with vigilant care; without ceasing on that account to be simple and natural in your whole demeanor; for the most vigilant are neither troubled nor embarrassed on account of their vigilance; yet excessive fear of being recreant either to duty or propriety in such like circumstances, would only expose you to greater danger of falling into the snare you try to avoid, as it would pre-occupy the mind and weaken the will. In such conjunctures, remain as near as possible to your mother, keeping your eyes fixed upon hers, always hearkening with a tender respect to the mysterious language that escapes from the maternal heart; a language easily understood by a daughter that loves the virtue of filial piety.

The mother's presence is always an infallible protection for young ladies; her looks are a book constantly open, and in which they can read her most secret thoughts; whether they approve or condemn their actions. Whenever you are called on to participate in worldly festivities let your mother be your visible guardian angel; she will preserve the innocence of your heart from the dangers that surround you. If you feel a secret desire to be relieved of your mother's presence, as being something noxious to your liberty, rest assured that your heart has already lost something of its innocence and simplicity. A daughter who dreads her mother's eye has evidently entered on a winding way, and ought to consider with suspicion the state of her soul. There is no company that you should prefer to that of your mother, no conversation that you should esteem more than hers; there should be no pleasure that could engage you to forego the pleasure of being near her. God himself has placed those sentiments in the hearts of young ladies in order to guard them against the seduction of the world and the attractions of false pleasures. He strengthens in their soul the virtue of filial piety, which forms an impregnable citadel around the heart, keeping it in perfect security against the evil influences of wicked agents.

Your conduct in every detail ought to be discreet and grave in the company of young men with whom you are unacquainted. If they speak to you, answer them briefly modestly and with simplicity, but fearlessly. Let it be your constant endeavor to converse on subjects capable of interesting a serious mind; in this way you can better divert their attention from frivolous topics, and prevent perhaps indiscreet questions or rash intimacies.

It is well to advert to the fact that, in consequence of a deteriorated faith and virtue among young men, in whom a bad education has oftentimes destroyed the happiest dispositions; many among them have lost that esteem, respect and veneration for woman so prevalent in the Christian ages prior to ours. Such, unfortunately, is the case in thousands of instances now-a-days; for when a young man finds himself in company with a young lady his chief object is to amuse himself with her, if his heart, already vitiated, does not entertain desires more criminal still; he is unguarded in his conversation, while displaying his talents, complimenting her for qualities which he interiorly believes her devoid of.

Bear in mind that this young man with whom you are conversing watches all your movements, studies all your looks, discusses and interprets interiorly every word you speak; while treating with you he plays the part of a cunning diplomatist whose wiles you happily ignore; but in order to escape from becoming his dupe, prudence should govern all your actions while in his company.

Remember that there are in the world manners, gestures and attitudes that constitute a conventional language, but which hold nothing in common with the genuine sentiments of the heart, being like a counterfeit money which vanity pays and receives. It is one of the most dangerous snares for a young girl whose simplicity and candor are yet intact. Those qualities, so precious in themselves, are sometimes prejudicial to her safety from the perfidy of a heart already skilful in the art of deceiving. For, judging others by her own heart, she cannot suspect those who converse with her of wicked designs. She accepts all that is told her as the sincere expression of the heart, and very often receives for a genuine affection what is only hypocrisy and deception.

If you are acquainted with the young men whom you meet in the world, you should know how to treat with them; yet experience proves that for the most part a young lady is little posted in matters of this nature. If the mind is already poisoned by the distemper of incredulity, if the heart is already vitiated, if they have justly won by their evil conduct a sad notoriety in the world, if they are of that class that seek to take the advantage of woman's simplicity by rendering vice agreeable to her in their own person; oh, you cannot treat them with too great severity. Your language, your looks, your attitude, should repel them from or command a respectful fear in your presence. Do not fear to wound their feelings, or to be impolite, or indecorous in their regard. An obstinate reserve, a severe demeanor, is all that you owe them. Treating them with that courtesy due to gentlemen would prove noxious to you, as they would not fail to make of it a plausible reason to justify their insolent conduct and rash judgments; be not deceived, the slightest mark of benevolence that they would receive from you would be immediately interpreted by them in the most perfidious manner. They detest virtue as much as you detest vice. They have a sovereign contempt for every woman, for they believe that she is unable to resist the allurements of pleasure.

They are mutual confidentials, and tell each other, with deplorable levity, all that young ladies innocently say to them; wickedly misconstruing their intentions, exaggerating what was true, and treating with sneering contempt those who were simple enough to believe in the sincerity of their hypocritical compliments. Most assuredly you have not the slightest desire of becoming the subject of the scandalous conversation of those men; you have but one means, however, of guarding yourself against their venomous tongue; that is, to exact from them a respectful deference by the gravity of your demeanor, and the severity of your relations with them.

If, on the contrary, you meet with young men who, with a lively faith, have conserved the purity of their hearts, and as a consequence of these virtues, all due respect for woman, you can show them greater confidence, and let them feel that you highly esteem them for their virtues, without, however, renouncing the precautions advised by prudence while in their company. It is in such encounters that your conversation should reveal a serious turn of mind, carefully avoiding every thing that would intimate undue confidence or intimacy; for the heart of a young lady should never be on her lips; except with regard to her mother, she should keep it buried in the depths of her soul to converse familiarly only with God and His angels.

CHAPTER XVII.
CURIOSITY.

CURIOSITY is a defect that seems to be particularly inherent to the heart of woman, and which, when not properly governed, never fails to entail the most disastrous consequences. Through it they have frequently acquired a knowledge of evil and a disgust for virtue. You are well aware that curiosity was the door through which sin and death enter the world; that when the devil sought our destruction he made use of woman's curiosity. Now, it is well not to lose sight of the fact that woman is always the daughter of Eve. She feels a pressing desire to see what pleases the mind, flatters the senses, and enlivens the imagination. Eager for vivid emotions, she seeks them with an insatiable avidity; and, rather than feel nothing, she prefers painful emotions, finding a certain secret charm even in the fits of sorrow and pains of her imagination. Her great desire to see and hear whatever tends to excite or create emotion is in a great measure the source of her curiosity. The education that women for the most part receive develops this disposition of the heart: an education which, instead of elevating the mind and giving it a taste for serious things, narrows it, and accustoms it to feed upon aliments that are trivial and void of consistency. The mind requires to he kept in constant activity, and since thoughts alone can do this they should be such as to amply furnish it with solid and wholesome food, for all kinds of thoughts are not equally good for it, no more than all kinds of food are equally good for the body. In some kinds of food the quantity and quality of nutriment are much inferior to what they are found to be in other kinds. Hence greater moderation is required in the use of the latter than in that of the former, otherwise the stomach, overcharged, would soon become disgusted with it.

On the other hand, no quantity of food void of nutritious qualities will ever appease hunger. The same thing may be said of the kind of thoughts with which the mind is fed; some are used less for their sound and wholesome nutriment than for their efficiency to flatter sensuality, inflame the passions, create new wants in the heart, and excite a depraved curiosity. Under this regime the mind is starved and tortured by an incessant hunger. It sadly languishes and pines in the grip of famine; and all this in the midst of full and plenty, but this abundance contains no nutriment, it is made up of news, whether true or false, which amuses without satiating; still the mind enlists the service of the senses to gather it up from all sides. The eyes, continually gaping and watching what passes before them, present the mind with numberless images to amuse it in its weary or lonesome moments.

Hence that insatiable thirst to see and observe every thing, that inconstancy and want of changing from one place to another, that desire to read useless and frivolous books, novels, weeklies and magazines, which for the most part enervate the mind by their futilities, trouble and darken it by a multitude of incoherent images and contradictory thoughts, and poison the heart by foul and filthy images that will constantly torment the soul.

The ears are on the alert to catch every report, every murmur, all kinds of news, detractions and calumnies, stories and scandals. I say all kinds of news, no--I make a mistake, it is only such news as is of an exciting or startling nature to break up the monotony of life. Hence those indiscreet questions which provoke answers more indiscreet still; those rash revelations made by thoughtless young ladies, those prying efforts to discover things which only exist perhaps in their own imagination, and of which they should live in holy ignorance.

Hence those long conversations, discussing the vices and evil doings of others, in which justice and charity are discarded, and iniquity drank like water. Few forego the criminal satisfaction of participating in those detestable conversations, and fewer still, alas! reproach themselves at night for the detractions and calumnies committed, permitted, or provoked during the day, and by a monstrous union they couple with those deeds the external practices of piety.

This is but a feeble picture of the frightful condition of a mind starved for want of solid and wholesome food, and poisoned by the empty frothings of vanity and passion. Curiosity is the constant companion of this mediocrity of the mind and poverty of the heart. In order to avoid this fatal rock, no pains should be spared, and if, unfortunately, you have already drank at its poisoned sources, hasten to use every available means to arrest its ravages. To insure success, do not amuse yourself with lopping off the branches of the evil, allowing the root to remain, do at once what is essential: feed your mind and heart with a genuine love for the true and beautiful.

A frivolous woman is invariably curious, and a curious woman always finishes by becoming the dupe and victim of her curiosity. To overcome an inordinate love for sights and news you must accustom the mind's eye to feast on the panoramic beauties of nature, and confine yourself to the company of persons of your own age, in whom you remark an elevated mind and heart,--lovers of what is truly good and grand.

Curiosity has its source, also, in another defect which becomes daily more and more prevalent--it is a want of forethought and reflection, arising from a volatile and frivolous mind. Few, indeed, are lovers of the interior life; all seem to be bent on parading the mind and heart, the imagination and senses. Now, when man has not learned the art of living and conversing with himself, he becomes wearisome and sometimes dangerous to himself when alone; because the mind, not knowing how to occupy itself, and not finding in its own resources the thoughts that elevate and nourish it, is obliged, in order to avoid lonesomeness, to dwell upon images which at least distract and weaken it, and not unfrequently disturb the peace of the heart.

Religion, always inspired by God in the choice and formation of the terms which it employs to convey the ideas that it wishes to impress upon the heart, has invented two words, which admirably express the meaning of the concentration of the faculties of the soul,--in other words, that society or cohabitation of man with himself--they are *self-composure and recollection.*

These words express that state or power of the will by which it holds complete control over all the faculties of the soul; so that sensibility can have no command over any of their operations. Thus shielded from this turbulent disturber they are enabled to labor peacefully and efficiently in their interior province or the soul.

The advantages secured by interior recollection are so great and the consequence of its absence so prejudicial that the Holy Ghost distinctly declares its absence to be the cause of all the evils that desolate the earth. *"With desolation is the earth laid desolate because there is no one who thinketh in his heart."* This is a terrible truth, but it is not the less real on that account. To be convinced of this you need only descend into your own heart, and you will soon discover that the want of interior recollection has been the cause of the most of your faults. It is during the interior composure of the soul's faculties that we understand what the Lord says. *I will hear what the Lord God will speak in me, for he will speak peace unto them that are converted to the heart.* (Psalm 84.)

But if we find nothing in the heart but trouble and obscurity we must naturally find many pretexts to justify our preoccupation with external things; and like a man, finding his house the abode of pain and displeasure, remains away from it as long as possible, we, too, will shun as far as possible the scene of our misery. It is, therefore, of most vital importance for you to form in your own heart an agreeable and useful society with which you can always converse. This society you carry with you wherever you go, for you are with yourself at all times; and since you have not always the satisfaction to enjoy the company of others you should learn how to turn to good account this privation by making it an incentive to cultivate with industry an agreeable society in your own heart; and the best way to insure the success of this work is to accustom yourself to converse with God who is always present in your heart, except when you expel him by mortal sin.

The work itself must be made up of pious readings, meditation and prayer, which will furnish you with such thoughts and affections as will prove to be constant friends in pain as in joy; hasten to amass these honeyed treasures during the noon-tide of life; for the winter will soon come upon you, the flowers of life shall lose their perfume and their withered corolla shall be strewn on the ground. Then you will not have time to enrich the soul with the longed-for booty when you will be reduced to the miserable condition of those women who endeavor to conceal the poverty of their mind and heart by a foolish and puerile deception.

CHAPTER XVIII.
MEDITATION AND REFLECTION.

Meditation and reflection are two words that express two shades of difference of the same idea. In meditation we consider supernatural things pertaining to our eternal salvation. The soul maintains herself with difficulty in the love and practice of virtue without the help derived from meditation; for when she gives it up, her fervor in piety grows lax, temptations became more frequent and obstinate, often followed by humiliating falls.

You are well aware that the real object of the Christian's life upon earth is to establish God's kingdom in our heart; and this is what forms the object of the second petition that we address to God every day in the Lord's prayer; and since the kingdom of God is entirely interior, as Jesus Christ himself tells us, when He says: **the kingdom of God is within us,** we should acquire the habit of looking for God in our own heart; but in order to find Him there we must give Him a place in it by meditation and prayer.

The advantages derived from meditation are so numerous and so great, that it is a matter of surprise why it is not more universally practised; for the effects that it produces in the souls of those who are faithful to its practice are so striking that it is easy to discern a man given to this habit from those who are entire strangers to its holy influence. Meditation teaches us to know God and ourself; it lays open to us our faults and vices, their source and fatal consequences and the arms we should employ to combat them. Finally, meditation contributes most efficiently to form our minds and purify our hearts, to fortify the will and develop in us the habit of reflecting.

The knowledge of God and ourself is such an important factor in the work of our spiritual perfection that St. Augustin constantly prayed for it, saying: *"Lord grant that I may know Thee and myself.*" The pagans themselves well understood the advantage of this most important science, even for the securing of the happiness of this life; since they had the following words inscribed, as a summary of all human science, upon the frontispiece of the most celebrated temple of Greece, **know thou thyself**. But, alas! this knowledge is as rare as it is necessary; with a mind absorbed by distractions, and a heart harassed by passions, we flee, so to speak, from God and from ourselves.

Where is the Christian that knows God? Do you presume that you know full well what He is, what He has done for you, and what He still does for you every day? Every moment you receive His gifts: your life is due to His beneficence and His love, you are carried in the bosom of His providence as in the arms of your mother, He is continually preoccupied with your welfare, He has done all, created all things for your comfort and happiness; for your sake he has become man, to participate in all the infirmities, weakness and miseries of our humanity, in order to heal them and console us. Every thing speaks of Him, and proclaims His holy name to you. All that you see, all that you hear and feel must recall to your mind some gift of His love, or some effect of His mercy. All creatures in heaven and on earth are like so many voices which, mingling in a harmonious concert, sing to you His praises and publish His mercies.

Do you listen to them? Do they not pass you unperceived like the flitting zephyrs' leaving no trace to mark their passage. Did you ever seriously try to render an account of the attributes of God, and particularly of His goodness and justice? of His goodness to endear Him to all, and of His justice to make Him be feared by all. Have you considered well that to know God is to know all, because He is the Author of all creation possessing in Himself to an infinite degree all the perfections of His creation?

He who does not labor to obtain a knowledge of God can scarcely obtain any knowledge of himself. How is it possible for us to know what we are while we ignore what God is for us and what we owe Him? Oh, how few there are who know themselves! The first condition necessary to secure this knowledge, so important and so precious, is profound humility, which unsparingly reveals the real motive of all our actions, the uncompromising antagonist of our pride and self-love.

Now it is quite evident that he who does not know God does not possess this virtue; for how can a man humble himself before a being that he ignores? At first sight it may seem that there is nothing so easy as to know one's self,--that this knowledge may be obtained by a close consideration of the heart's operations; but when we give the matter sufficient thought the work does not appear to be so easy. And the number of those who have acquired this knowledge to any noted degree is so limited that we are forced to infer that a knowledge so rare must offer great difficulties.

However, there is one thing certain, namely: that this knowledge is not obtained in the midst of tumult and pleasures, from the seductions of the world or the distractions of life. It is not by fleeing one's-self as we would fly an enemy; by concealing with a complaisant but perfidious veil our defects, to avoid being troubled by their appearance--always painful to pride; it is not by living a dreamy life of fiction to which the slaves of the world condemn themselves with a deplorable obsequiousness; it is not by continually trying to deceive ourselves and others that we may learn how to know ourselves; and, just as our knowledge of material things increases by the frequency of our relations with them--for instance we know persons better with whom we are intimately acquainted than those with whom we are comparatively strangers--so, likewise, in order to know ourselves well, we must live intimately with ourselves, observe closely and impartially all the movements of our mind and heart, frequently descending into the depth of our soul, scrupulously examining our thoughts, desires and actions, sparing no pains to discern well their source and motives; this latter portion of the work is, without doubt, the most difficult, since it is the point at which all the passions unite to deceive us by the most subtle illusions. The best actions are despoiled of their merit by certain motives of vanity, often concealed from our own notice.

The motives by which we are actuated are, relative to our actions, what the eye is relative to our body,--it is the motive that gives light and brilliancy to our actions. This is the sense in which we should understand our Lord when He says if our eye be simple our whole body will be luminous. Now the great light by which we can clearly see the motives for which we act is meditation.

In the peaceful calm of solitude, and in the silent slumber of the passions, meditation puts us in presence of ourselves, before our own eyes, by which we see ourselves as in a true mirror. Meditation teaches us to judge without prejudice what we have done and to determine with propriety what we should do, by making the experience of the past our lamp for the future, and by converting past mistakes into practical lessons for the present.

The meditative and recollected soul will turn even her shortcomings to good account; seeing her delinquencies, she clothes herself with the mantle of humility, she rises with renewed confidence, and shuns with greater care the occasion of those evils from which she has suffered; she is rarely taken by surprise, a few moments' reflection will suffice for her to determine what is to be done under the circumstances; she is rarely taken in the snare of deception, for she knows that human nature is weak, vacillating and unreliable, and, consequently, she keeps herself on her guard.

Considered from this point of view; meditation is particularly necessary to woman, because, being endowed with a very lively imagination and a tender heart, she is more exposed to illusions which, for the most part, spring from those two sources. Moreover, surrounded as she is, by the seductions of the world; breathing incessantly the poisoned atmosphere of flattery and adulation; waited on by men who seek to deceive her; distracted by a multitude of cares which absorb her soul; lost in a painful detail of trifles; how will she be able to resist the united action of those trials; if she has not contracted the salutary habit of frequently conversing with her own heart by holy meditation and recollection?

The precious habit of meditation makes its influence felt by all the faculties of the soul. It imparts to the mind the love of solitude, assurance and confidence to the judgment, consistency to all the thoughts. It is by reflecting on what we interiorly feel, as well as on what we exteriorly see, that we enrich our intelligence and acquire that cheerful alacrity and firmness of purpose so necessary and precious in the most trying and delicate circumstances of life.

A woman of an irreflective mind becomes an easy prey to her own impressions; rarely ever seeing things in their true light she is balloted from one illusion to another, from one error to another; she believes in every thing, hopes for all that she desires, and desires all that flatters her. Unable to render an exact account either of the thoughts of her mind or the movements of her heart, she acts without aim or motive, governed solely by the caprice of her imagination or the impulse of whimsical humor; equanimity is impossible in the midst of such confusion. All this will have a fatal effect upon her spiritual welfare; for what shocked her some time ago will now fail to make the slightest impression. The bloom of youth will soon fade away, leaving to her only confused souvenirs of those days when, to be happy, it sufficed for her to descend into her own soul, where she always found peace and consolation.

If you wish to preserve in all their integrity the faculties of your soul; if you would not have your life ruled by the caprice of the imagination; contract at an early age the salutary and happy custom of making your meditation. Set apart a special time for it every day, let it be practical, having for its object the spiritual progress of your soul, the sanctification of your life. Lay out in God's presence what you have to do every day, recall to mind the places, persons and things that have been to you an occasion of sin, or a help in the exercise of virtue, in order to avoid the evil accruing from the one source, and increase the influence arising from the other. Never recline your head upon your pillow before having rendered an exact account of the day you have just finished, like the merchant who, every night, tots up his loss and gain, to see what has been the result of the day's transactions. The next day, with the double armour of experience and resolve, you will be better able to avoid what proved noxious before, as well as to do the good that you had omitted. By thus acting you will give to your life a sure direction, a powerful impetus in the accomplishment of all that is worthy of your glorious destiny.

CHAPTER XIX.
OBEDIENCE TO PARENTS.

In the natural order of things, man, after having obeyed his parents in his youth, becomes in turn the head of another family which he must govern by the authority of his word and example. God has given to woman another vocation. She obeys from her childhood, and obedience becomes more necessary to her as she advances in years; for when she quits the paternal roof for the one of her choice, it is still to obey and be directed by the will of another. But in this second moiety of her life she often finds the practice of obedience more difficult and painful than it was when she lived with her parents. More than once has the young woman, allured by the deceitful charms of a false liberty, left with a secret joy the paternal roof, hoping thereby to be delivered from the duty of obedience which weighed so heavily on her heart. But, alas! she has often been obliged to regret those days as the happiest of her life, when the tender solicitude of a mother rendered submission sweet and easy.

God, whose Providence is infinitely wise, has disposed all things in such a way that each epoch of life is a preparation to that which follows; strengthened by the labors of the past, we are fitted for those of the future, and prepared for the accomplishment of the duties of to-day by our fidelity to obligations less difficult of yesterday; we are thus imperceptibly and safely conducted by this graded scale to the end for which we were created.

Hence you may consider the present as your noviciate to the future; the family circle at home is the image of that with which you must live at a later time; and while your duties and trials will vary with your position, there is one obligation that always remains invariable; that is obedience. If you have learned well how to obey your parents whom God has given you, you will find it easier in after life to bend your will when obliged in submission to that of another.

At present holy obedience is not painful to you; on the contrary, it is a pleasure, as it is a means by which you can please your dear parents whom you love; and by force of habit it is now so deeply engraved in your heart as to be an act of second nature. But other times and other circumstances will present new difficulties, when perhaps you will be obliged to obey a man of your own age, possessed of none of those qualities that give authority and prestige to command.

The familiarity that exists between the married couple which, when truly Christian, is one of the greatest charms of their life, not unfrequently becomes for woman an obstacle to the observance of obedience; but she has reason to rejoice when her delinquency does not diminish the sacred authority of her husband's commands. The lady who has been docile to the orders of her parents will be docile to those of her husband; for as we are assured by Holy Writ, our accomplishment of the duties that God has imposed on us relative to our parents is rewarded even in this life; as likewise our delinquencies on this point will incur heaven's displeasure.

The paternal home should be for you a school of respect, obedience, gratitude, and love; and these virtues should be constantly manifested in your conduct; for, mark it well, you will be in the position destined for you later by God what you are presently in that which you now occupy. There is a logical succession in all our actions, whether good or bad. In each one of your actions may be found the germ of another which, being developed in due time, will produce others. The same is also true of that happy or unfortunate succession of thoughts and affections which is developed into habit; and which is engrafted in our very souls, forming, as it were, an integral part of our nature. From our infancy, God, in His infinite goodness, has given us a facility to do good, which in the course of time can be strengthened by habit; it will enable us to surmount obstacles and dangers that increase with age, but which are ignored in childhood.

The individual practice of respect, obedience, confidence; and gratitude is necessary for the preservation of society; and in order to render this practice easy for us, God, in loving goodness has removed from those beautiful flowers of virtue, whose perfume should embalm our whole life, the thorns that might pierce us. He has confided their care to those to whom, after God, we owe our life, and towards whom we are drawn by an invincible inclination of the heart. When we merge into the noon-tide of life we find these virtues already engrafted in our souls, with little trouble to us, for they were planted there by the hands of good and pious parents; and, as a reward for our fidelity to their instructions, those cherished virtues take deep root in the heart and grow imperceptibly as we advance in years.

But if, instead of being docile to their orders, we have stubbornly resisted them, if, by some unaccountable egotism, the soul has become concentrated in herself; and instead of giving our confidence and love to those who have so generously given their life and means to secure to us the happiness we enjoy, we rest satisfied with living on the fruits of their labors without making them any return; we will carry with us later on into the family of our choice only a withered heart, dead to every noble and generous sentiment.

You should respect and honor your parents with the filial love of a Christian daughter. Such is the precise meaning of the precept given you by God in their regard: *Honor thy father and thy mother!* Relative to you they hold God's place, who is the source of all paternity in heaven and upon earth. Nothing can dispense you from this respect which God requires for them, and which nature ought to render easy to you; for, even when your parents would suffer by a criminal negligence the image of God to be deteriorated in their souls; they always remain His representatives for you, because they are always, no matter what they may do, the instruments that God employed to give you existence.

The faults of your parents should never diminish in your heart the respect and honor that you owe them; and in certain painful and delicate circumstances, you should imitate the example of the two sons of Noah in order to escape the malediction that fell upon Cham for his impudent strictures of his father's faults. You should carefully draw the mantle of charity over any fault of your parents that might tend to weaken your respect for them. Silence should seal your lips forever on all their shortcomings, even before those who know them, unless that it be to ask advice in some critical conjuncture, or bring them to receive some useful and charitable counsel. God alone should be the depository of your sorrowful confidence in this matter. To Him alone you should confide your sorrows and alarms, because He alone should hold the first place in your mind and heart, for He will be your judge as well as theirs.

If you see that a salutary effect may be obtained by a prudent and respectful observation, be slow in making it, and never act before having consulted some virtuous and enlightened persons; should they advise you in the affirmative, let your observation assume the tone of a remonstration rather than a warning. Your language, actions or gestures should never savor of anything that betrayed a disregard for that profound veneration with which you should honor in them the title of God's representatives in your regard. An unfortunate custom, the fruit of a bad education, or of an excessive tenderness on the part of parents, has sadly vitiated the nature and form of the relations that should exist between child and parent.

During the present century in many places a fatal familiarity seems to have sapped the very foundation from that profound respect which was the honor and glory of the Christian family, and the salt that preserves nations from corruption; that respect which children, who truly feared God, paid to their parents. To that beautiful order that reigned in the Christian family, and which preserved inviolable the father's authority in Christian times, has succeeded a spirit of equality as hostile to the natural order as to the order of Divine Providence, since it destroys both rank and duty. It gives birth to that false independence which may justly be called the seed of revolution and anarchy; no consequence is more natural, for what can be expected of a citizen who imbibed in his childhood, under the paternal roof, the spirit of disobedience and insubordination, who was taught to regard superiority with a jealous eye, and treat with contempt those who are beneath him.

After paying due respect to your parents, they should be, after God, the depositories of your confidence, and since a daughter's wants are more easily communicated to her mother, it is in her mother's heart that a Christian daughter will deposit the secrets of her own. This filial confidence supposes, also, in a young lady a sincere diffidence in her self, a consciousness of her own weakness which, so far from being a fault, is the result of true humility. Those young ladies who are wanting in confidence in their own mothers are indeed great objects of compassion. For this confidence is not only an essential condition to their advancement in virtue, but also one of their principal safeguards against deception and intrigue.

The heart of woman, especially at your age, feels an imperative need of making a confidant of some one, and if that one is not her mother, it will be some friend who, perhaps, will not possess greater experience nor more wisdom or force than herself, and consequently, instead of giving the proper counsel, will add evil to evil by the fatal help of encouragement in a course that should be abandoned. Rest assured that you can never find any one able to fill the mother's place in this regard. This unreserved abandonment to a mother's confiding heart is not always possible, since death often interferes. When such is the case it is a great misfortune for a young lady--a misfortune that can scarcely be retrieved in her lifetime. It is easy to recognise a woman whose soul has been fostered in that of her mother. Such women ordinarily possess a milder disposition, a more amiable ingenuousness, with a certain simplicity of heart which, without being prejudicial in the least to her mind, adds a new charm to the noble and generous virtues which become the mother of a family. Those habits of confidence and abandonment contracted from childhood have made frankness and sincerity second nature. Their love for truth and sincerity is revealed in their conversation, the sanctity of which is the echo of their souls. Their whole demeanor sheds such a halo of delight around them that they become, unpretentiously, the centre of attraction for all those whose enviable pleasure it is to be honored by their company.

If up to this hour you have concealed nothing from your mother; if you have given her the key to your soul; if your heart is for her an open book; if she can at all times read in your looks your very thoughts; on bended knees thank God from the depths of your soul for having given you such a mother, and the grace of giving her your confidence. If you remain a child to your mother you will preserve your youth through the toilsome days of life to a ripe old age, an advantage so precious that nothing should be left undone to secure it.

Woman is pleasing to others only in as much as she possesses this adornment, which exhales a sweet odor like the perfume of youth. Alas! how many women there are who have never been children even with their mothers. Women from their youth, they have treated their mother with a kind of diffidence, dissembling at an age when the only danger to be feared should be an excessive confidence.

As for the gratitude and love that you owe your parents, I would regard it as an injury offered to the candor of your age and the sincerity of your heart to undertake to prove that these are obligations which you are in duty bound to discharge. God who has commanded us to honor our parents, left us no precept obliging us to love them; but while He engraved other commandments upon stone this one He has written in the very essence of our being. Hence I appeal only to your heart in this matter, leaving you entirely to its instincts to point out to you your duty, which to assert by any other proof, I fear would lead you to suspect that there are children unnatural enough to forget and neglect their parents.

Bear in mind, however, that your love and gratitude for them must by no means be restricted to a sentiment of the heart or an instinct of nature. Those virtues must find an echo both in your words and actions. Love founded on sensibility has no signification, if you can make no sacrifice to obey or please them. Love in man is effective, and this is why our Lord tells us with regard to the love we owe Him: *He who loves me keeps my commandments.*

To love consists in pleasing him who is loved; it is prefering his will to our own, his interests to ours; in a word, it is to seek him rather than attract him; it is to become his property rather than to appropriate him; it is to forget ourself to think of him. Love lives upon sacrifices; as the pious author of the Following of Christ says: *where love is, there is also pain: but love converts that pain into pleasure.* If this be true of all the affections of the human heart; what shall we think of the one that we have first felt, and which in some way forms a part of our very nature?

CHAPTER XX.
MELANCHOLY.

I t will perhaps seem strange to you to be warned in the bloom of youth against a sentiment that seems to be reserved for that period of life when delinquents, through the infinite goodness of God, are brought to enter into themselves; when the illusions of the heart have been replaced by a cold and sad reality; when hope seems to recoil under the weight of sad recollections. Still, because this mental canker preys on the most vital interests of the soul, and because a predisposition to it is found to prevail even among the youthful portion of your sex, a certain knowledge of it is necessary in order to resist it effectually.

It is most delightful and consoling to find in persons of your age and sex that pure joy, so frank and candid, springing out of the innocence and simplicity of the heart; a good conscience and a lively faith, with unbounded confidence in Divine Providence; all of which combine to produce that sweet and saintly cheerfulness which dilates the heart and lights up the soul with its amiable reflections. But, alas! we confess with deep regret, that many young ladies have been ruthlessly robbed of all those charms by a precocious development received under the world's tutorship, by which they have been made to cross with a bound the smiling season of hope and joy, to a premature old age before having tasted the charms of youth.

In order that joy may reign in the heart, the heart must first repose in the bosom of Divine Providence--free from the pressure of doleful souvenirs, and from the pestering desires stirred up by vanity; in a word, exempt from every obstacle, whether intrinsic or extrinsic, that might in any way oppose the designs of God. But, alas! by some unaccountable inconsistency, we are in contradiction with ourselves; for, notwithstanding our great desire to live, and our horror of death, still we seem to be in a hurry with the time to pass, as though we advanced too slowly to the grave.

Now, we are well aware that of this lifetime the present is all that we can claim, the past and future being in the hands of God; still, true to the same principle of inconsistency we make little or no use of the present, it is something annoying that we wish, to get over, as quickly as possible, while we are absorbed by a countless multitude of useless but importunate desires relative to the past, which we can never recall, and the future, which perhaps we shall never see.

Hence, as we journey onward in this way, we must naturally find ourselves a prey to fears and doubts, sometimes suspended between hope and despondency, while the heart is harassed by corroding desires that succeed each other like waves on a tempest-driven sea. We wish to be our own providence, to dispose of our own future of our lifetime according to those desires, instead of leaving that work to Him from whom we have received all that we possess.

When we are assailed by regrets in the evening, and filled with anxieties for the morrow, how can our heart rebound with joy, or our lips wear the smile of confidence and tranquility? Behold some of the many sources from which the fatal fiend of melancholy is fed and strengthened. But this vile destroyer of peaceful joy springs from another source not less fatal than those just mentioned. That is a certain vagueness of mind and heart, which is sometimes the result of some physical or bodily indisposition, but more frequently the consequence of an imperfect education, or indifference in the service of God.

That which gives to the mind its needed assurance and strength, and to the heart its consistency and solidity, is a lively faith, nourished and sustained by a sincere piety. Of this you are thoroughly convinced, as you know full well that faith alone can give a solid basis to our thoughts, a true direction to our desires, and an eternal destiny to our hopes. Without faith the mind is without ballast--unsettled as to what it ought to believe or reject; the heart ignores what it should fear or hope for; in a word, the soul is lost in the midst of her vacillating desires.

In order that faith may impart its vivifying influence it must penetrate the soul's substance, and become to her the principle of a new life, directing all her movements, animating all her thoughts, desires and hopes. A superficial and inactive faith that is purely exterior, satisfied with believing what God reveals, without quickening the spiritual pulsations of the soul, will not preserve her from that vagueness and uncertainty which deprive all objects of their natural colors, and lend them a sombre shade which saddens the heart.

If you would escape falling a victim to melancholy, preserve your faith with precious care, enliven it constantly by fervent prayer, by meditation and the abundant graces received through the Sacraments. Let its pure light be the rule of your thoughts and actions, accustom your mind to dwell upon things that are practical, and consequently useful, sedulously avoiding all speculative or doubtful topics, that have no other result than to keep the mind in a state of suspense and indecision. You will fare better in having a clear knowledge of practical things, even at the cost of appearing less learned than others.

A third source of melancholy is a species of mental idleness, concerning which women are exposed to labor under a false impression. As they are naturally given to manual occupation habit begets with them an antipathy to mental labor; their judgment is readily but erroneously convinced by their feelings, which easily lead them to believe that they are sufficiently occupied when their fingers are engaged in fixing an embroidery or something similar. To reason the matter, they will readily admit that labor exclusively manual having no share in the exercise of the mental faculties, cannot be considered to give sufficient occupation to an intelligent being; since the imagination would be left to the mercy of its caprices and the heart to the whims of its desires, which is not worthy of a being created to the image and likeness of God, who commands us to labor as He labored, namely: with mind and heart constantly supplying useful thoughts to the one and noble sentiments to the other.

Such is the heavenly duty enjoined by those consoling words of our Saviour: *pray always*. At first sight it would seem that such an obligation is impossible and contrary to human nature. We cannot, however, even suppose that He who has made man what he is, misunderstood his nature so far as to command him to do impossibilities.

Every thought that raises the mind towards God, every sentiment that brings the heart near to Him, is a prayer. Hence there is no occupation that may not become a prayer, since there is none that may not be referred to God. The duties and obligations of woman, far from being an obstacle to the practical exercise of the above principle, on the contrary favor its execution most admirably; for her duties, though of the manual order for the most part, are not of a nature to distract the mind or absorb the heart; she can easily and constantly concentrate the thoughts of the one and the affections of the other upon God.

That you should make God the object of all your actions is your first and most imperative duty, and the moment that you discharge your duties for any other end that moment they shall lose the dignity of deeds worthy of a Christian or even of a rational being; moreover, your mind, as you are fully aware, is endowed with perpetual activity, it is never idle,--you need only chose the objects to which you wish to apply it. But if you fail to apply it to things worthy of your sublime calling it will soon escape from your control, and, flitting from one trifle to another, it will meddle with objects that might become dangerous to the peace of your soul. It will soon become preoccupied by puerile fears, unfounded apprehensions, vague sadness, which, when constantly indulged in, will deliver your soul over to melancholy which never fails to tarnish the purity of the heart and enervate the energy of the will.

The pain that many suffer from their imaginary ills robs them of the noble and generous love of compassionating the real and painful griefs of others. Egotism is nurtured and fortified in those ravings which attach the soul's energies to the consideration of our own ills or sorrows; the heart grows cold and hardened in a deplorable insensibility which estranges it to every sentiment of pity and compassion for others.

There is, I am aware, a sorrow that is salutary to the soul, and conformable to the spirit of Christianity, as also to man's condition in this vale of tears. I know that it is very difficult to be always joyful, when we take into account the dangers by which we are surrounded, the countless calamities to which we are exposed since the day that sin had entered the world. We very often see the objects of our warmest affections disappear from around us; and every day some new misfortune or some new loss adds some new tears to our cup of sorrow, from whose bitterness every one is doomed to drink during life.

Far from me be the thought of engaging you to fly this holy sorrow imposed by our condition and recommended by our Lord Himself. *"There is,"* says St. Paul, *"a sorrow according* to God" which, far from plunging the heart into a state of despondency, enables the soul to avoid the dangers which constantly expose her to lose God by sin. But this sorrow does not trouble the peace of either the heart or the mind, for it is that sorrow which our divine Saviour called blessed, and for which He has promised consolation.

Far be from me, also, the thought of advising that foolish and boisterous joy which carries away the soul, absorbing all her energies filling her with void and disgust. This joy, far from being a remedy or a protection against melancholy, is, on the contrary, both its cause and effect. The result of those intemperate paroxysms of joy, so little in conformity with our nature is that which invariably results from any forced or undue influence.

When shackled nature recovers her liberty she revenges the violence that she was made to endure. But, seizing her rights with too great avidity, she suffers more from the reaction than from the force that infringed upon them. This explains the reason of those fitful outbursts of joy and grief that pass in quick succession. Those puerile fears, followed by hopes, without rule or aim, that vain confidence giving place to sad discouragement. Those despondent feelings after moments of zealous fever, during which we seem to be able to do and attempt everything. Here we find the solution of those sudden and varied shades of temperament which will instantaneously cheer or prostrate the energies of the soul.

If you would preserve your soul from melancholy, conserve your heart in a calm composure, your mind in a just equanimity keeping both equally distant from all extremes able to taste joy with discretion, and sorrow without becoming discouraged. This will be putting in practice the advice of the wise man: Give not up thy soul to sadness and afflict not thyself in thy own counsel. The joyfulness of the heart is the life of man and a never-failing treasure of holiness, and the joy of man is length of life. Have pity on thy own soul, pleasing God and contain thyself; gather up thy heart in his holiness and drive away sadness far from thee. For sadness hath killed many and there is no profit in it. Envy and anger shorten a man's days, and pensiveness will bring old age before the time. A cheerful and good heart is always feasting, for his banquets are prepared with diligence. Eccl. xxx. 22-27.

CHAPTER XXI.
ON READING.

If the wisdom of nations, which loves to find expression in the proverbs, teaches us that a man may be known by knowing the company that he frequents; we can say with the same assurance that his character and dispositions may be known from the books which he constantly reads. Of all friends, the most intimate are the books that we constantly read, hence there is nothing more important for a young person, as there is nothing that entails such grave consequences for the moral culture, than the selection of proper and suitable books. Because it is a noted fact that such readings exercise the deepest influence over the mind and heart, so much that all the resources which the ingeniousness of maternal love can employ against it avail nothing. God's minister in the pulpit of truth has no weight with those souls fascinated by the deceitful charms of a bad book, which addresses itself to their prejudices and passions. The charitable advice of the confessor in the tribunal of penance is futile against the intoxicating seductions of those romances whose only merit consists in flattering the most depraved inclinations of the human heart.

Indeed it is a subject both of surprise and sorrow to see an author of the most menial abilities lauded to the skies for a book still more abject than himself, a book teeming with error and immorality; while, very often, a discourse, a sermon or an instruction, whatever may be the authority that they receive either from the character of the person who pronounces them, or from the gravity of the circumstances in which he speaks, are heard with indifference. Good and evil, truth and error, are never so rapidly propagated, never so powerful in their action, never so certain in their effects as when they are communicated to us under the form of a book authorized by fashion or party spirit. Hence there is no greater responsibility before God than that which man assumes when he wields the pen in the name of humanity, whether for noble or selfish ends.

A book is a teacher whose doctrine is listened to with a willingness equal to its degree of conformity to the inclinations of our heart. It is a friend that gains our confidence, inasmuch as it flatters our prejudices and passions, and in which we find a reflection of our own thoughts, the echo of our most secret sentiments. You would not like to receive a stranger into your house without his being properly recommended, but you will readily receive a book on the strength of reports that are often deceitful.

The country is flooded with productions that sap the foundations of morality, and which bear that *imprimatur* given by a poisoned public opinion to such authors as pander to its craven spirit. The world judges with a depraved indulgence the book in which it finds its maxims approved and sanctioned, portraying the exact seducing picture of its vanities. The purest souls and, not unfrequently, serious minds are too often imposed upon by those popular prejudices, and, despite their good reason, yield to their influence by reading the flimsy productions of depraved minds, which, besides all the other injuries they cause, rob them of a most precious time. A book must be very bad before the world condemns it, so bad, in fact, that its own intrinsic filth disgusts the reader and seals its fate. But, there is another kind of literature favorably received by that portion of mankind called respectable, honest, and sometimes even severe, and whose authority is capable of making a grave impression on your mind.

It is, therefore, very important for you to know not only the signs by which to recognize a bad book, but also whom you should consult as judges in the matter. There can be no question here of those books professedly immoral, in which vice is eulogized and corrupt maxims sustained. Those books are not dangerous for you, because they will not fall under your hands, and even when they would you could not open one of them without flinging it away with horror;--in this case the evil-- contains in itself its own remedy.

But there are books, less dangerous in appearance, in which the most delicate situations are represented, clothed in all the charms of style, well calculated, under their moral guise and serious bearing, to captivate the heart and imagination. Indeed to represent in lively colors the terrible effects of the passions, and the fatal consequences that a momentary excitement might entail is not of a nature to inspire a young lady with horror for vice and love for virtue. How is it possible that she will guard against the evil inclinations of the heart, when she is conscious of the danger in giving them free scope, and that a momentary forgetfulness is sometimes punished by a life-time of sorrow and bitterness? Such a culpable negligence might be accounted for, if there existed a necessary relation between the will and the imagination, by which the determinations of the former are necessarily dependant upon the impressions of the latter.

But such is not the case, for the imagination has a sphere of action very different from that of the intelligence or the will. It is an interior mirror which reflects back upon the soul images of things beheld by the senses and conceived by the intelligence, without regard to time or place. Positively no, would be the answer of a young lady of self-respect, whom we would ask if she would like to see with her own eyes all that is spoken of in the novel which she reads with so little caution! Your answer would be given in the same terms, should we ask you if she might read without impunity to virtue those intrigues, those scenes so engaging to curiosity, and which incite the reader to follow up the details of ineffectual struggles against passion. Could she, without blushing, listen to the passionate conversations of those who had lead each other to destruction, after having exhausted all the resources of heart and mind to render vice amiable, even when their fall would seem to be less the effect of a criminal will than the result of a kind of fatality? Your answer to all this would be emphatically, no!

But while young ladies will neither listen to nor look at scenes of this nature, many, alas! do not scruple to look at them in books, where they are much more dangerous, for being adorned with all the charms of style, and because the persons represented are made to speak and act in a much more luring manner than they do in reality. They devour with avidity those dangerous, and sometimes scurrilous pages; but while they chain their attention to the matter they are reading, their imagination gains the ascendancy over all the senses, and under their united action images are formed which leave a lasting impression on the mind--images of misfortune that has befallen persons either through their own fault or the fault of others, and which, through sympathy, the human heart, whether wrong or right, is always ready to find a pretext to justify.

In reading of those misfortunes she may perhaps recognize the hand of divine vengeance pursuing the criminal culprit, which is of a nature to inspire her with a sentiment of fear that deters from the commission of crime; but such sentiments have been felt by the heroes of the novel which she has read, and nevertheless they have fallen into the abyss which they so much dreaded, I would almost say while fleeing from it. But when they take their stand on a declivity so steep and slippery, nothing short of a miracle can save them.

Such is precisely the nature of the danger in which the readers of such books place them-selves. In those books human frailty is idolized, deeds committed through it are either necessary or excusable, the hair-breadth escapes, and often the tragical conclusion of their story, will often inspire the reader with a salutary terror, it is true; but will that feeling destroy all those tender sympathizing sentiments that were felt while dreading it? Of course this fear is felt by the will, but the imagination has already finished its work; it has seen, heard and felt by the senses; it has delighted and fascinated the soul by those images whose charms cannot be destroyed by the unfortunate issue of those struggles in which frailty played such an important role.

The will, distracted by the tumult of external things, and the variety of, her occupations or pleasures, will soon lose this sentiment of terror on which she seems to count so much, but the imagination will conserve for a long time the impressions and images upon which it has feasted, and which will form the constant subject of her thoughts during the day and of her dreams during the night.

Hence, the books that are capable of producing such results are evidently bad, and if you wish to preserve intact the innocence of your heart you should never take one of them in your hands. If you wish to conceive a deep horror for vice, and guard against the snares of passion, you will more readily and securely attain your end by reading a few serious books in which truth is presented in its own simplicity without artifice. Books in which the author, realizing the importance of his mission, directly addresses the mind without trying to captivate the heart and imagination, or to render vice amiable first in order to inspire you with horror for it afterwards. If you wish to be true to yourself; if by your readings your object is to cultivate a love for virtue and horror for evil, novels are not the books that you will have recourse to.

Hence, to draw a practical conclusion from our considerations on this subject, you may safely say that a book is, if not bad, at least dangerous when its tendencies are to render interesting, and agreeable such deeds or language as you would neither look at nor listen to. This should be the first rule by which to judge of the moral worth of the books you wish to read.

CHAPTER XXII.
SAME SUBJECT CONTINUED.

To the rule given in the foregoing chapter may be added another of equal importance in the selection of suitable books to read. Generally speaking, all books that draw too much on the imagination may be considered as dangerous. You are well aware, and it has been frequently said, in the course of this little book, that the imagination is precious and useful when regulated with discretion, and directed with prudence; but the moment that it is allowed to assume a preponderance which does not belong to it, it becomes noxious to our spiritual and temporal welfare. Moreover, it is united to the senses by the most intimate ties, through which it receives impressions and images that keep it in constant activity; we should constantly labor to check, rather than to encourage its development; while we should spare neither pains nor diligence to develop the intelligence which, when left in ignorance of truths that could enlighten and elevate it, becomes the victim of cruel doubt, idleness, effeminacy and pleasure.

There are books said to be useless, and consequently harmless, but the conclusion, without being false, is not just; for we have just as much reason to believe they are dangerous as to admit the contrary. Now, if a book is indeed useless you cannot bear to read it, and since you do read it, it must certainly contain something interesting which renders it agreeable to you; it pleases some faculty of your soul, some habitual thought of your mind, some predominating disposition of your heart.

That a book may be read without profit is quite true. But that the same book can be read without danger of sustaining some loss is evidently false, unless that it be maintained that we are justified in having no proposed end for our actions; or that we may act solely for pastime which is diametrically opposed to the end for which we were created: Our time is too precious to be used indifferently. Again if there is in life anything that may be read or omitted without losing some advantage, or committing some evil, it is certainly not a book, for it always contains either some facts or some pictures, or some maxims capable of making an impression on your mind and heart.

The intelligence is formed and developed by means of language, and language, considered from this point of view, furnishes us with no idle words. Hence a useless book is, in the true acceptation of the term, a book that amuses the imagination and the heart. Now, whatever the soul receives through these channels must be of some importance for good or evil. Hence we are not justified, on the plea of indifference to accept any book that falls under our hands without being thoroughly examined and competently recommended.

Here, of course, a new difficulty occurs: at your age, and with your experience, you are unable to judge what books you should read; you are therefore obliged to follow the advice of others in the matter, but not the advice of all indiscriminately, as all are not competent to direct you in a matter of such grave importance. Popularity will give a wide circulation to a book bat can by no means recommend it; hence public opinion is not a rule that will guarantee you against deception.

Those in whom you place entire confidence to choose a book for you should themselves be recommended by their sincere and generous piety, the dignity of their life, the solidity of their judgment, strengthened by an extensive knowledge of men and things. Above all things be on your guard against the books recommended by worldly women, lovers of pleasure and parties; those whose light and frivolous minds sicken at serious thoughts, who are on their guard lest they may do too much for God, and who vainly endeavor to reconcile, in a monstrous union, the maxims of the world with those of the Gospel, the seductions of pleasure with the austerities of virtue, desiring to serve God and mammon.

If, by some negligence, or even in good faith; you open one of those books against which you have been warned, shut it the moment you feel your imagination excited by the images it offers, or when you perceive that the mind's curiosity becomes aroused to its agreeable narration of incidents, for it is almost always an unfavorable sign of a book that produces those and similar effects. Such is not the manner in which truth and virtue affect us. Their action is milder and calmer, and has the heart and will, rather than the imagination for its object. Hence, be on your guard, lest by some indiscretion you allow a poison to enter your soul, which is never more dangerous than when it seems least to be feared.

Finally, to resume in a few words, all that we have considered on the subject: If you would place the moral merit of a book beyond question, ask yourself if you would like to have its author for your spiritual director; do not think that this precaution is exaggerated or uncalled for; for between the author of a book and the reader there are relations established so intimate that they beget a kind of intellectual paternity, which produces deeper and more durable effects than you may be aware of.

To express the influence that our actions exercise over our life and over our fate, man is said to be the son of his works. For similar reason, it may be said of him, but more especially of woman, that he is the son of his readings, for reading forms such an important factor in the formation of the heart and mind that it often modifies our whole being. Besides, if you wish to profit by your reading, read only a few books, but read them well, with close attention, reflecting long and often on what you have read, identifying your very thoughts and sentiments with the subject matter of their pages. But let all this have its practical utility, let all those advantages find a living expression in your language, in your actions, and in your whole life.

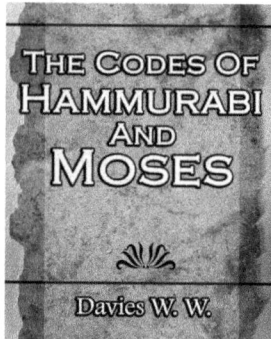

The Codes Of Hammurabi And Moses
W. W. Davies

QTY

The discovery of the Hammurabi Code is one of the greatest achievements of archaeology, and is of paramount interest, not only to the student of the Bible, but also to all those interested in ancient history...

Religion   **ISBN:** *1-59462-338-4*   **Pages:132**

MSRP $12.95

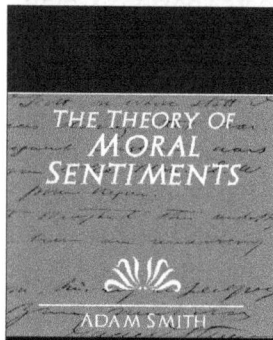

The Theory of Moral Sentiments
Adam Smith

QTY

This work from 1749. contains original theories of conscience amd moral judgment and it is the foundation for systemof morals.

Philosophy   ISBN: *1-59462-777-0*   **Pages:536**

MSRP $19.95

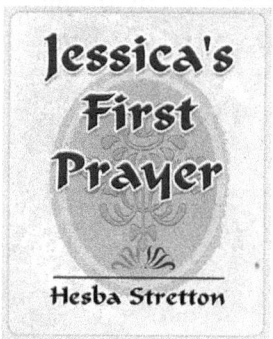

Jessica's First Prayer
Hesba Stretton

QTY

In a screened and secluded corner of one of the many railway-bridges which span the streets of London there could be seen a few years ago, from five o'clock every morning until half past eight, a tidily set-out coffee-stall, consisting of a trestle and board, upon which stood two large tin cans, with a small fire of charcoal burning under each so as to keep the coffee boiling during the early hours of the morning when the work-people were thronging into the city on their way to their daily toil...

Pages:84

Childrens   ISBN: *1-59462-373-2*   *MSRP $9.95*

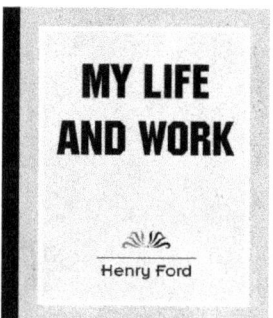

My Life and Work
Henry Ford

QTY

Henry Ford revolutionized the world with his implementation of mass production for the Model T automobile. Gain valuable business insight into his life and work with his own auto-biography... "We have only started on our development of our country we have not as yet, with all our talk of wonderful progress, done more than scratch the surface. The progress has been wonderful enough but..."

Pages:300

Biographies/   ISBN: *1-59462-198-5*   *MSRP $21.95*

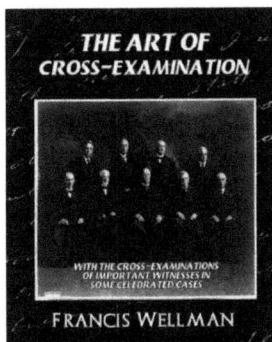

The Art of Cross-Examination
Francis Wellman

QTY

I presume it is the experience of every author, after his first book is published upon an important subject, to be almost overwhelmed with a wealth of ideas and illustrations which could readily have been included in his book, and which to his own mind, at least, seem to make a second edition inevitable. Such certainly was the case with me; and when the first edition had reached its sixth impression in five months, I rejoiced to learn that it seemed to my publishers that the book had met with a sufficiently favorable reception to justify a second and considerably enlarged edition. ..

Reference   ISBN: *1-59462-647-2*

Pages:412

MSRP $19.95

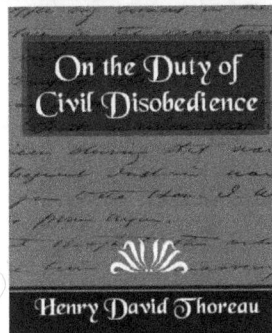

On the Duty of Civil Disobedience
Henry David Thoreau

QTY

Thoreau wrote his famous essay, On the Duty of Civil Disobedience, as a protest against an unjust but popular war and the immoral but popular institution of slave-owning. He did more than write—he declined to pay his taxes, and was hauled off to gaol in consequence. Who can say how much this refusal of his hastened the end of the war and of slavery ?

Law   ISBN: *1-59462-747-9*

Pages:48

MSRP $7.45

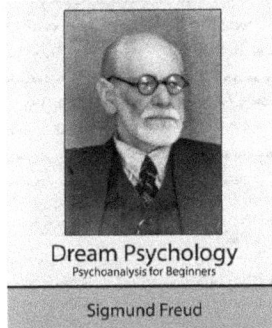

Dream Psychology Psychoanalysis for Beginners
Sigmund Freud

QTY

Sigmund Freud, born Sigismund Schlomo Freud (May 6, 1856 - September 23, 1939), was a Jewish-Austrian neurologist and psychiatrist who co-founded the psychoanalytic school of psychology. Freud is best known for his theories of the unconscious mind, especially involving the mechanism of repression; his redefinition of sexual desire as mobile and directed towards a wide variety of objects; and his therapeutic techniques, especially his understanding of transference in the therapeutic relationship and the presumed value of dreams as sources of insight into unconscious desires.

Psychology   ISBN: *1-59462-905-6*

Pages:196

MSRP $15.45

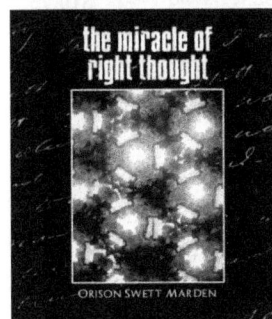

The Miracle of Right Thought
Orison Swett Marden

QTY

Believe with all of your heart that you will do what you were made to do. When the mind has once formed the habit of holding cheerful, happy, prosperous pictures, it will not be easy to form the opposite habit. It does not matter how improbable or how far away this realization may see, or how dark the prospects may be, if we visualize them as best we can, as vividly as possible, hold tenaciously to them and vigorously struggle to attain them, they will gradually become actualized, realized in the life. But a desire, a longing without endeavor, a yearning abandoned or held indifferently will vanish without realization.

Pages:360

Self Help   ISBN: *1-59462-644-8*   *MSRP $25.45*

The Rosicrucian Cosmo-Conception Mystic Christianity by *Max Heindel*　ISBN: *1-59462-188-8*　**$38.95**
The Rosicrucian Cosmo-conception is not dogmatic, neither does it appeal to any other authority than the reason of the student. It is; not controversial,
but is: sent forth in the, hope that it may help to clear..　　　　　　　　　　　　　　　　　　　　　　New Age/Religion Pages 646

Abandonment To Divine Providence by *Jean-Pierre de Caussade*　ISBN: *1-59462-228-0*　**$25.95**
"The Rev. Jean Pierre de Caussade was one of the most remarkable spiritual writers of the Society of Jesus in France in the 18th Century. His death took
place at Toulouse in 1751. His works have gone through many editions and have been republished...　　　　　Inspirational/Religion Pages 400

Mental Chemistry by *Charles Haanel*　ISBN: *1-59462-192-6*　**$23.95**
Mental Chemistry allows the change of material conditions by combining and appropriately utilizing the power of the mind. Much like applied chemistry
creates something new and unique out of careful combinations of chemicals the mastery of mental chemistry...　　　　　New Age Pages 354

The Letters of Robert Browning and Elizabeth Barret Barrett 1845-1846 vol II　ISBN: *1-59462-193-4*　**$35.95**
by *Robert Browning and Elizabeth Barrett*　　　　　　　　　　　　　　　　　　　　　　　　Biographies Pages 596

Gleanings In Genesis (volume I) by *Arthur W. Pink*　ISBN: *1-59462-130-6*　**$27.45**
Appropriately has Genesis been termed "the seed plot of the Bible" for in it we have, in germ form, almost all of the great doctrines which are afterwards
fully developed in the books of Scripture which follow...　　　　　　　　　　　　　　　　Religion/Inspirational Pages 420

The Master Key by *L. W. de Laurence*　ISBN: *1-59462-001-6*　**$30.95**
In no branch of human knowledge has there been a more lively increase of the spirit of research during the past few years than in the study of Psychology,
Concentration and Mental Discipline. The requests for authentic lessons in Thought Control, Mental Discipline and...　New Age/Business Pages 422

The Lesser Key Of Solomon Goetia by *L. W. de Laurence*　ISBN: *1-59462-092-X*　**$9.95**
This translation of the first book of the "Lernegton" which is now for the first time made accessible to students of Talismanic Magic was done, after careful
collation and edition, from numerous Ancient Manuscripts in Hebrew, Latin, and French...　　　　　　New Age/Occult Pages 92

Rubaiyat Of Omar Khayyam by *Edward Fitzgerald*　ISBN: *1-59462-332-5*　**$13.95**
Edward Fitzgerald, whom the world has already learned, in spite of his own efforts to remain within the shadow of anonymity, to look upon as one of the
rarest poets of the century, was born at Bredfield, in Suffolk, on the 31st of March, 1809. He was the third son of John Purcell...　　Music Pages 172

Ancient Law by *Henry Maine*　ISBN: *1-59462-128-4*　**$29.95**
The chief object of the following pages is to indicate some of the earliest ideas of mankind, as they are reflected in Ancient Law, and to point out the
relation of those ideas to modern thought.　　　　　　　　　　　　　　　　　　　　　　Religiom/History Pages 452

Far-Away Stories by *William J. Locke*　ISBN: *1-59462-129-2*　**$19.45**
"Good wine needs no bush, but a collection of mixed vintages does. And this book is just such a collection. Some of the stories I do not want to remain
buried for ever in the museum files of dead magazine-numbers an author's not unpardonable vanity..."　　　　　Fiction Pages 272

Life of David Crockett by *David Crockett*　ISBN: *1-59462-250-7*　**$27.45**
"Colonel David Crockett was one of the most remarkable men of the times in which he lived. Born in humble life, but gifted with a strong will, an
indomitable courage, and unremitting perseverance...　　　　　　　　　　　　　　　Biographies/New Age Pages 424

Lip-Reading by *Edward Nitchie*　ISBN: *1-59462-206-X*　**$25.95**
Edward B. Nitchie, founder of the New York School for the Hard of Hearing, now the Nitchie School of Lip-Reading, Inc, wrote "LIP-READING Principles
and Practice". The development and perfecting of this meritorious work on lip-reading was an undertaking...　　　　How-to Pages 400

A Handbook of Suggestive Therapeutics, Applied Hypnotism, Psychic Science　ISBN: *1-59462-214-0*　**$24.95**
by *Henry Munro*　　　　　　　　　　　　　　　　　　　　　Health/New Age/Health/Self-help Pages 376

A Doll's House: and Two Other Plays by *Henrik Ibsen*　ISBN: *1-59462-112-8*　**$19.95**
Henrik Ibsen created this classic when in revolutionary 1848 Rome. Introducing some striking concepts in playwriting for the realist genre, this play
has been studied the world over.　　　　　　　　　　　　　　　　　　　　Fiction/Classics/Plays 308

The Light of Asia by *sir Edwin Arnold*　ISBN: *1-59462-204-3*　**$13.95**
In this poetic masterpiece, Edwin Arnold describes the life and teachings of Buddha. The man who was to become known as Buddha to the world was
born as Prince Gautama of India but he rejected the worldly riches and abandoned the reigns of power when... Religion/History/Biographies Pages 170

The Complete Works of Guy de Maupassant by *Guy de Maupassant*　ISBN: *1-59462-157-8*　**$16.95**
"For days and days, nights and nights, I had dreamed of that first kiss which was to consecrate our engagement, and I knew not on what spot I should
put my lips..."　　　　　　　　　　　　　　　　　　　　　　　　　　Fiction/Classics Pages 240

The Art of Cross-Examination by *Francis L. Wellman*　ISBN: *1-59462-309-0*　**$26.95**
Written by a renowned trial lawyer, Wellman imparts his experience and uses case studies to explain how to use psychology to extract desired information
through questioning.　　　　　　　　　　　　　　　　　　　　How-to/Science/Reference Pages 408

Answered or Unanswered? by *Louisa Vaughan*　ISBN: *1-59462-248-5*　**$10.95**
Miracles of Faith in China　　　　　　　　　　　　　　　　　　　　　　　　Religion Pages 112

The Edinburgh Lectures on Mental Science (1909) by *Thomas*　ISBN: *1-59462-008-3*　**$11.95**
This book contains the substance of a course of lectures recently given by the writer in the Queen Street Hall, Edinburgh. Its purpose is to indicate the
Natural Principles governing the relation between Mental Action and Material Conditions...　　　New Age/Psychology Pages 148

Ayesha by *H. Rider Haggard*　ISBN: *1-59462-301-5*　**$24.95**
Verily and indeed it is the unexpected that happens! Probably if there was one person upon the earth from whom the Editor of this, and of a certain previ-
ous history, did not expect to hear again...　　　　　　　　　　　　　　　　　　　Classics Pages 380

Ayala's Angel by *Anthony Trollope*　ISBN: *1-59462-352-X*　**$29.95**
The two girls were both pretty, but Lucy who was twenty-one who supposed to be simple and comparatively unattractive, whereas Ayala was credited, as
her Bombwhat romantic name might show, with poetic charm and a taste for romance. Ayala when her father died was nineteen... Fiction Pages 484

The American Commonwealth by *James Bryce*　ISBN: *1-59462-286-8*　**$34.45**
An interpretation of American democratic political theory. It examines political mechanics and society from the perspective of Scotsman
James Bryce　　　　　　　　　　　　　　　　　　　　　　　　　　　Politics Pages 572

Stories of the Pilgrims by *Margaret P. Pumphrey*　ISBN: *1-59462-116-0*　**$17.95**
This book explores pilgrims religious oppression in England as well as their escape to Holland and eventual crossing to America on the Mayflower, and
their early days in New England...　　　　　　　　　　　　　　　　　　　　　History Pages 268

www.bookjungle.com *email: sales@bookjungle.com fax: 630-214-0564 mail: Book Jungle PO Box 2226 Champaign, IL 61825*

QTY

The Fasting Cure *by Sinclair Upton* ISBN: *1-59462-222-1* **$13.95**
In the Cosmopolitan Magazine for May, 1910, and in the Contemporary Review (London) for April, 1910, I published an article dealing with my experiences in fasting. I have written a great many magazine articles, but never one which attracted so much attention... New Age/Self Help/Health Pages 164

Hebrew Astrology *by Sepharial* ISBN: *1-59462-308-2* **$13.45**
In these days of advanced thinking it is a matter of common observation that we have left many of the old landmarks behind and that we are now pressing forward to greater heights and to a wider horizon than that which represented the mind-content of our progenitors... Astrology Pages 144

Thought Vibration or The Law of Attraction in the Thought World ISBN: *1-59462-127-6* **$12.95**
by William Walker Atkinson *Psychology/Religion Pages 144*

Optimism *by Helen Keller* ISBN: *1-59462-108-X* **$15.95**
Helen Keller was blind, deaf, and mute since 19 months old, yet famously learned how to overcome these handicaps, communicate with the world, and spread her lectures promoting optimism. An inspiring read for everyone... Biographies/Inspirational Pages 84

Sara Crewe *by Frances Burnett* ISBN: *1-59462-360-0* **$9.45**
In the first place, Miss Minchin lived in London. Her home was a large, dull, tall one, in a large, dull square, where all the houses were alike, and all the sparrows were alike, and where all the door-knockers made the same heavy sound... Childrens/Classic Pages 88

The Autobiography of Benjamin Franklin *by Benjamin Franklin* ISBN: *1-59462-135-7* **$24.95**
The Autobiography of Benjamin Franklin has probably been more extensively read than any other American historical work, and no other book of its kind has had such ups and downs of fortune. Franklin lived for many years in England, where he was agent... Biographies/History Pages 332

Name	
Email	
Telephone	
Address	
City, State ZIP	

☐ **Credit Card**   ☐ **Check / Money Order**

Credit Card Number	
Expiration Date	
Signature	

Please Mail to: Book Jungle
PO Box 2226
Champaign, IL 61825
or Fax to: 630-214-0564

ORDERING INFORMATION
web: *www.bookjungle.com*
email: *sales@bookjungle.com*
fax: *630-214-0564*
mail: *Book Jungle PO Box 2226 Champaign, IL 61825*
or PayPal *to sales@bookjungle.com*

Please contact us for bulk discounts

DIRECT-ORDER TERMS

**20% Discount if You Order
Two or More Books**
Free Domestic Shipping!
Accepted: Master Card, Visa,
Discover, American Express

www.ingramcontent.com/pod-product-compliance
Lightning Source LLC
Chambersburg PA
CBHW081234090426
42738CB00016B/3296